Hand-Building Techniques

Joaquim Chavarria

WATSON-GUPTILL PUBLICATIONS/NEW YORK

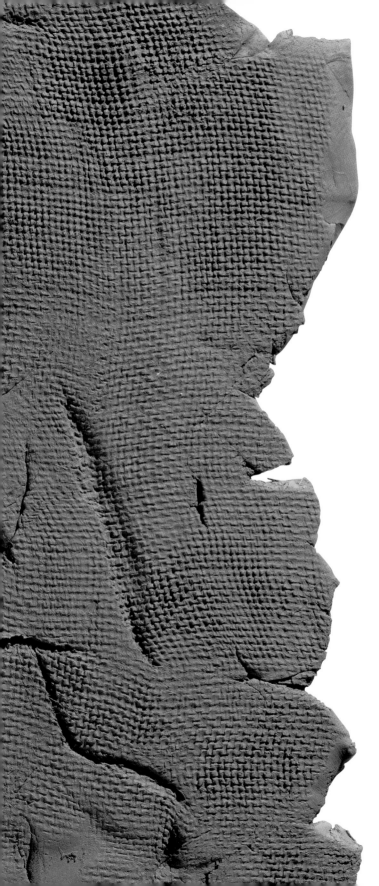

Ceramics Class: Hand-Building Techniques
Original Spanish title:
    Aula de céramica: Modelado
Editorial director: María Fernanda Canal
Production director: Rafael Marfil
Text and exercises: Joaquim Chavarria
Graphic Design: Carlos Bonet
Diagrams: SET, Serveis Editorials i Tècnics
Dummy: Pedro González
Photography: Nos & Soto
Archive research: Mª Carmen Ramos
Translation: Mark Lodge

First published in the United States in 1999 by Watson-Guptill
Publications, a division of VNU Buisness Media, INC
770 Broadway, New York, N.Y. 10003-9595
www.watsonguptill.com

Copyright © 1998 Parramón Ediciones, S.A.
Ronda de Sant Pere, 5, 4th Floor
08010 Barcelona. Spain

Library of Congress Catalog Card Number: 98-83065
ISBN 0-8230-0591-7

Manufactured in Spain

CONTENTS

INTRODUCTION

The practice of modeling clay by hand is one of the most ancient technical processes. The use of this material to produce pots goes back to the beginnings of humankind. It is easy to imagine our ancestors observing the footprint of some animal, or even their own prints, in the mud. Engrossed in his role as hunter, prehistoric man probably did not imagine the possibilities suggested by such a material. Prehistoric woman, though, upon approaching a lake to fetch water, saw her prints in the lime. She may well have bent down to make a hand print, realized the possibilities, and then begun to make use of the material that was present in abundance near the rivers and lakes where they were camped.

The women, who were already familiar with the technique of basket weaving, may have covered the interior of a basket with clay as an experiment. They would then have seen that the results were good, especially after the clay had dried, making the basket firmer. Later came the firing technique, perhaps accidentally discovered when one of these clay-lined baskets was left near the fire. When the clay was heated, the people realized that it had turned into an entirely different sort of material, harder and waterproof, allowing for storage of liquids.

From this moment on, working with clay became the norm. Those first basket "models" were repeated entirely in clay, pinching the pots in the same way used to cover the insides of the baskets. The pottery produced was mainly used to store and cook food.

Nothing incites the imagination more than necessity. From the pinching method primitive peoples moved on to other techniques, such as punching the fist into a mass of clay and turning the mass to raise and build the walls. They also formed ropelike coils by rolling the clay under their hands and used these coils as a basis for building pots. Until the invention of the potter's wheel, these two systems were used to create all the pottery we know. In societies that did not develop the potter's wheel, these two methods continued to be used. The method of hand-building solid pieces was also known, used for making small votive figurines that represented deities and were used in religious rituals.

Using only these methods of hand-building, people could create any type of pot, although other methods also emerged, such as building with strips or with slabs. This book uses each of the hand-building methods to create a series of pieces. This is only a small part of the medium's potential. Some of these examples are very traditional in their methods; others less so. I have included them to encourage beginners to move beyond copying the traditional approach to imagine other possibilities as well.

With practice you will reach the point where you can tell which method is best suited to carrying out a particular idea. With further experience and knowledge you will be able to achieve very creative, unique pieces using the same basic processes.

My best wishes to all of you.

Chavarria

Joaquim-Manuel Chavarria Climent

PROPERTIES OF CLAY

Clay comes from the feldspar abundant in the Earth's crust. Water passing through the rock erodes it, dissolving the soluble materials and depositing them in layers.

Clays can be divided into two types: primary and sedimentary (or secondary). Primary clays are found in the same area as the rock from which they originated. They have thick particles, little plasticity, are very pure and white, and may be fired at high temperatures. Kaolin is a primary clay.

Sedimentary clays are those that were transported far from the rocks from which they originated by water or glacial action. Such clays have been ground by water into particles of different sizes. The first to be deposited are the heavier particles, then the medium ones, which are carried further by the water, and finally the finest particles, which continue to dissolve in the water until it stops flowing and becomes stagnant. Sedimentary clay is finer and more plastic than primary, but it may contain impurities consisting of other minerals or organic matter. These impurities may lower the clay's firing temperature and alter its color.

The basic mineral of which clay consists is kaolinite, or hydrous silicate of alumina composed of alumina (aluminum oxide), silica (silicate oxide), and water. Thus the chemical formula is $Al_2O_3.2SiO_2.2H_2O$, in proportions of approximately 40 percent alumina oxide, 46 percent silica, and 14 percent water.

Plasticity

When moist clay is modeled, its plasticity allows the particles to slide over one another and hence to keep the shape it is given. Highly plastic clays absorb large amounts of water and increase in volume. If the water absorption is too high, the clay will lose plasticity and will become too soft and sticky because the particles will have lost adherence capacity. If a piece of clay is saturated with water, it is best to let it dry partially before using it.

Clay should be allowed to rest for a time after being prepared and reaching the correct moisture level. This aging period makes the clay more plastic, a quality that will increase after kneading.

To test the plasticity of a piece of clay, first make a ball and then flatten it into a coil. Make a small arch and check to see if the surface is completely smooth. If there are cracks, it means the clay is not very plastic and will have to be mixed

From top to bottom: red earthenware; white industrial earthenware; gray industrial earthenware; porcelain; stoneware; stoneware with fine grog; stoneware with medium grog.

with another, more plastic clay before use.

Shrinkage

When clay absorbs water, it become softer and its volume increases. But when this moist clay is exposed to the air for a time, it becomes hard and loses volume as it dries. This process is called shrinkage, or contraction. Drying occurs by capillary action, which causes the water to travel from the interior to the surface, where it evaporates.

Clays that absorb lots of water will shrink more. The more plastic types of clay will also shrink more than less plastic ones. During the drying process, the particles of clay come closer together due to the loss of water. The size of the particles also influences the degree of shrinkage. Thus clays with smaller particles will shrink more than those with larger particles.

Mixing opening (or non-plastic) materials with clay can speed the drying process since they won't absorb as much water.

Pieces that have been dried at room temperature still contain moisture. They can only dry completely in the kiln at 100°C (212°F), the boiling point of water, but even then only the water in a liquid state will have been eliminated. The water that is chemically fused with the clay will only disappear at 550°C (1022°F). At this temperature, an irreversible change (a chemical reaction) occurs in the structure of the clay, transforming it into a harder material. Thus the contraction of clay occurs in two stages, during drying and then during firing.

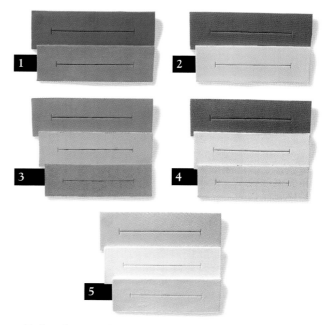

1. Red earthenware: bisque-fired at 1000°C (1832°F).
2. Gray industrial earthenware: bisque-fired at 1000°C (1832°F).
3. Stoneware: bisque-fired at 1000-1250°C (1832-2282°F).
4. Stoneware with fine grog: bisque-fired at 1000-1250°C (1832-2282°F).
5. Porcelain: bisque-fired at 1000-1300°C (1832-2372°F).

TYPES OF CLAY

Various types of clay are used in ceramics, including ball clay, stoneware, industrial earthenware, refractory clays, red earthenware, betonite, andkaolin.

Ball clays. These sedimentary clays fire easily and are very plastic. Often mixed with kaolin in the preparation of ceramic body, they cannot be used alone because they are too plastic and become sticky when they come in contact with water. They shrink to about 20 percent of their original size and vitrify at 1300°C (2372°F), serving to improve the plasticity of other clays (Figure 1).

Stoneware clays. These are both plastic and refractory. Their temperature of vitrification is 1250–1300°C (2282–2372°F). Feldspar acts as a fluxing agent. Their color after firing can vary from a very light to a dark gray, or from tan to brown (Figure 2).

Industrial earthenware clays. These are very white after firing (900–1050°C /1652–1922°F) and are used in the preparation of ceramic body. They should have very little iron oxide (less than 1 percent), or the color will turn from white to ivory (Figure 3).

Refractory clays. These are very resistant to heat and have a high melting point (1600–1750°C/2912–3182°F). Kaolinite and alumina are present in these clays in elevated percentages. They are quite pure, with little iron oxide. After firing, their color varies from cream to gray (Figure 4).

Red earthenware (ferruginous) clays. These contain a high percentage of iron oxide. They are highly plastic and fire easily. They can withstand temperatures of up to 1100°C (2012°F), but melt at higher temperatures and can be used as a glaze for stoneware. When wet, these clays are red, turning a reddish-brown after drying and becoming darker and darker as they reach their maximum firing limit (Figure 5).

Bentonite. This highly plastic volcanic clay contains silica and alumina and is added to ceramic body to increase plasticity. When it comes in contact with water, it can increase 10 to 15 times in size. It fires at about 1200°C (2192°F). Its chemical formula is $Al_2O_3.4\ SiO_2.9H_2O$ (Figure 6).

Kaolin (china clay). This primary clay is the principal component in the preparation of ceramic body for porcelain. It is white in color both before and after firing. It fires at 1800°C (3272°F), though if mixed with feldspar, the vitrifying point falls. It can be added to industrial earthenware clays to increase their heat resistance. Its plasticity is so low that it can't be modeled, but it can be used with molds (Figure 7).

OTHER MATERIALS

A. Chalk
B. Quartz
C. Dolomite
D. Feldspar
E. Grog
F. Talc

Clay is mixed with other materials when preparing ceramic body. Some of these reduce the plasticity by reducing their shrinkage during drying; these are called nonplastic or opening materials. Others reduce the temperature of vitrification; these are called fluxing agents. Ceramic body may contain bentonite, kaolin, calcium carbonate, quartz or silica, grog, dolomite, feldspar, or talc.

Calcium carbonate (chalk). This fluxing agent reduces the vitrification temperature of a ceramic body for low to medium firing. Its vitrifying power is very high if added in proportions greater than 13 percent, at which concentrations it may cause the piece to deform or melt. White in color, it is extracted from limestone and marble and has a high melting point. The chemical formula is $CaCO_3$. It is common in almost all clays (Figure A).

Quartz. Quartz is added to ceramic body as an opening agent, reducing shrinkage and increasing thermal expansion. This helps glaze fuse with the ceramic body. It is white and melts at 1600°C (2912°F). The chemical formula is SiO_2, or silicon dioxide, an anhydride combination of silicon and oxygen (Figure B).

Dolomite. Bicarbonate composed of calcium and magnesium, dolomite acts as a fluxing agent in ceramic body and can substitute for calcium carbonate. It is added to porcelain body in a ratio of 2 percent. It contains about 31 percent calcium oxide and 20 percent magnesium oxide; formula is $CaCO_3.MgCO$ (Figure C).

Feldspar. Formed through the erosion of granite and igneous rocks, feldspar is commonly used in hard earthenware bodies, as well as in stoneware and porcelain. It acts as an opening material, reducing the shrinkage of pieces during drying. It also acts as a fluxing agent at temperatures above 1200°C (2192°F). Feldspar can be divided into two groups: sodium-potash feldspars and calcium-sodium feldspars. Their formulas are potash feldspar (orthoclase): $K_2O.Al_2O_3.6$ SiO_2; sodium feldspar (albite): $Na_2O.Al_2O_3.6SiO_2$; calcium feldspar (anorthosite): $CaO.Al_2O_3.2SiO_2$; nepheline syenite: $K_2O.3Na_2O_4.Al_2O_8.SiO_4$ (Figure D)

Grog. Grog consists of bisque-fired clay ground to different-sized particles: coarse, medium, fine, and super fine (wherein the material resembles a powder). Color varies according to the type of clay from which it is made; white clays, for example, yield white grog. Grog is fired at higher temperatures than the ceramic body to prevent its contraction during firing. It is an opening material and thus speeds the drying of a piece and increases its resistance to heat during firing. It is very useful in ceramic body to be used for sculptures and wall murals because it decreases shrinkage during drying. If used in proportions of 30–40 percent, its texture will be noticeable in the piece (Figure E).

Talc. Talc is a hydrous magnesium silicate containing about 64 percent silica and 32 percent magnesium. It acts as a fluxing agent in ceramic body with a low firing temperature but high resistance to heat and should be added at a ratio of 2 percent. It consists of pulverized steatite, a very soft stone also known as soapstone or tailor's chalk. It is a very fine, powdery material that does not mix easily with water. It should be mixed with other materials in a dry state (Figure F).

CLAY MIXTURES

Ceramic bodies are composed of precisely calculated mixtures of different types of clay and other substances. To prepare a ceramic body, these ingredients are necessary:

- The clays, which are the plastic component
- Silica and grog, opening materials that reduce shrinkage and provide smooth drying, preventing warping or cracking
- Feldspar and calcium carbonate, the fluxes, which control hardness and firing time

Certain naturally occurring ceramic bodies can be used without modification, except for removing impurities and adding the necessary water. The ceramic bodies used to make all types of ceramic pieces can be natural or prepared, and they can be fired either once or twice after drying. In the former case, single firing, the glaze is applied to the dried piece before firing, and then placed in the kiln. The temperature is raised until the glaze fuses with the piece. In the latter case, a preliminary firing, called bisque firing, is done, at temperatures of 900–1000°C (1652–1832°F), after which the piece is glazed and fired again until the glaze matures.

Mixture Types

Ceramic body can be classified in two groups: porous (not vitrified) and vitrified. The first group includes clay mixtures with a high iron content, as well as white industrial earthenware. The second includes stoneware and porcelain clay bodies.

Red earthenware. These red clay bodies have a high iron content. They are very plastic and commonly used for hand-building and throwing. Firing temperature is 950–1110°C (1742–2030°F). The formula is 60 percent red earthenware clay, 30 percent kaolin, and 10 percent silica; or 85 percent red earthenware clay and 15 percent refractory clay (Figure 1).

White industrial earthenware clays. These are white or ivory and do not contain iron. They are vit-

rified or glazed after a first firing. There are three types of industrial earthenware clays: hard, mixed, and soft (Figure 2).

Bisque-firing tempertures for hard earthenware clays are 1180–1300°C (2156–2372°F), although they are not stoneware. Vitrifying temperatures are 1050–1180°C (1922–2156°F). The preparation formula is 50 percent kaolin, 40 percent quartz or silica, 8 percent feldspar, and 2 percent chalk.

Mixed clay is bisque-fired at 1050–1180°C (1922–2156°F), and then vitrified at 1000–1110°C (1832–2030°F).

Soft earthenware clays are fired both times at temperatures of 960–1080°C (1760–1976°F). The preparation formula is 48 percent ball clay, 34 percent silica, 12 percent kaolin, and 6 percent chalk.

Stoneware clays. After firing, these clay mixtures become nonporous, vitrified, and opaque. They are fired at 1150–1300°C (2102–2372°F); the resulting color can be gray, ivory, beige, or brown. Porosity should be less than 3 percent. The preparation formula is 40 percent potash feldspar, 30 percent refractory clay, and 30 percent kaolin, with a firing temperature of 1250°C (2282°F); or 50 percent refractory clay,

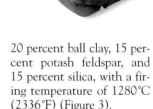

20 percent ball clay, 15 percent potash feldspar, and 15 percent silica, with a firing temperature of 1280°C (2336°F) (Figure 3).

Porcelain mixtures. These ceramic bodies are pure white, vitrify, and are translucent when less than 3 mm (1/8 in.) thick. Firing temperatures are 1250–1460°C (2282–2660°F). Kaolin is the principal component, but they also contain feldspar as a flux and quartz. There are two types of porcelain: soft and hard. The soft porcelain is less resistant and is fired at 1250–1300°C (2282–2372°F). Its formula is 54 percent kaolin, 26 percent potash feldspar, 18 percent quartz, and 2 percent bentonite, firing at 1250°C (2282°F). Hard porcelain is a highly resistant clay mixture and is fired at very high temper-

atures, 1380–1460°C (2516–2660°F). Its formula is 50 percent kaolin, 25 percent potash feldspar, and 25 percent quartz, with an approximate firing temperature of 1450°C (2642°F) (Figure 4).

Bone china. Bone china is mainly composed of calcinated bones (calcium phosphate), which act as fluxing agents. After firing, it is a hard, translucent, fine white clay. Its firing temperature is 1200–1250°C (2192–2282°F). The formula is 48 percent calcinated bones (calcium phosphate), 28 percent potash feldspar, and 24 percent kaolin.

Refractory clays. These fire at high temperatures, above 1600°C (2912°F). They do not contain iron oxide, which would lower the firing temperature, and are very hard, withstanding thermal blasts without deterioration. Their color after firing is variable. They are used in the ceramics industry to produce special bricks, crucibles, kiln bats, and insulating material. To reduce shrinkage, they are mixed with 40–60 percent grog from carboniferous schist clays (petrified clays) that have been ground and fired.

PREPARING CLAY MIXTURES

Even if you use prepared ceramic body instead of mixing it yourself, it is useful to know something about how to produce a mixture, which may ultimately help you develop your work more fully.

Specialized stores sell a variety of clay mixtures, both in dry and wet states, as well as the components for individual preparation. The wet clays are ready for use and come in packages weighing about 10–12 kg (20–25 lbs), hermetically sealed in plastic bags to prevent the clay from drying out. Prepared dry mixtures and the powdered materials necessary for preparing such mixtures often come in sacks of about 40–50 kg (75–100 lbs.).

The following illustrations demonstrate how to prepare a stoneware body from dry ingredients according to the formula of 40 percent potash feldspar, 30 percent refractory clay, and 30 percent kaolin.

1. With a small iron sledge hammer, break up the chunks of dry stoneware clay into little bits.

2. Crush the small bits into powder with a rolling pin.

3. Sift this powder through a 30-mesh sieve.

4. Weigh the sifted powder on a set of scales. The weight of the powder must be known to calculate the amount of water needed. The total weight of the dry body is 6 kg.

5. Measure the correct amount of water (450 cc of water per kg of clay powder) in a graduated test tube and pour it into a clean plastic container.

6. Sprinkle the clay powder into the water slowly; try to avoid lumps. The powder quickly sinks to the bottom.

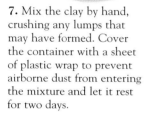

7. Mix the clay by hand, crushing any lumps that may have formed. Cover the container with a sheet of plastic wrap to prevent airborne dust from entering the mixture and let it rest for two days.

8. Pour the clay mixture onto a 60-mesh sieve placed over another plastic container. Push the mixture through the sieve with a gloved hand and a rubber spatula.

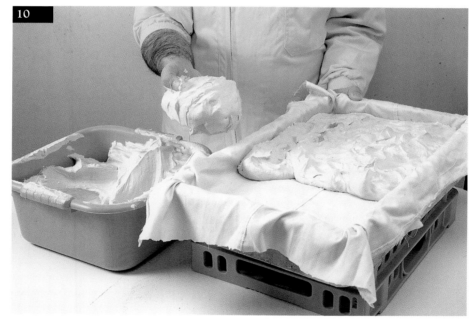

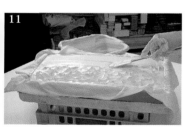

9. Cover a melamine-coated wooden frame with a clean cloth. Place the wooden frame on a slab of plaster and place this on a plastic crate to allow the plaster slab to be aerated from underneath.

10. Fill the frame with the clay. The cloth prevents particles of plaster from entering the mixture.

11. Using the rubber spatula, smooth the surface of the mixture to allow it to dry evenly. Any parts jutting out from the main mass should be smoothed off, since these would dry faster, creating hard, dry particles that would cause problems when kneaded into the clay later.

12. Leave the mixture in the frame for 48 hours. During this time, the plaster slab will absorb some of the water, causing the clay mixture to become more compact.

13. The body is ready to be kneaded. After kneading, it is best to allow it to age for at least one month before using it. Remember that aging increases the plasticity of clay.

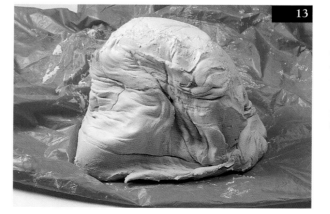

MATURING TEMPERATURE AND POROSITY

Maturing temperature

Ceramic body prepared by the potter should be tested before use. One of the fundamental tests is to ascertain its maturing temperature by using the following procedure. Prepare a small amount of clay; knead it to the proper moisture point, then with a rolling pin create three or four flat rectangular pieces measuring about 15 x 3 x .5 cm (6 x 1 1/4 x 1/4 in.). Allow them to dry between two plaster slabs or two bisque-fired tiles to prevent warping. Once dry, place each of them on two triangular stands in a tray made of a known clay to catch any melting clay from the samples in case of overfiring, thus preventing the bats in the kiln from being ruined. Place the trays in the kiln and fire the samples at the temperature estimated to be correct according to the components of the mixture. After firing, check the state of the samples: are they in good condition or have they undergone undesirable changes? The condition can be assessed by observing the samples' color, hardness, porosity, the sound made when tapped, and whether deformity has occurred. A sample found to be very porous is underfired; the next sample should be fired at a temperature 50°C (106°F) higher, and so on until the right porosity is attained. By the same token, if the sample is overfired, fire the next few samples at temperatures that decrease by 50–100°C (106–212°F) until you find the right temperature.

The table below explains the different states of three fired clay samples.

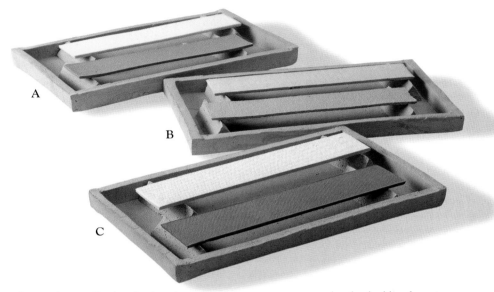

The condition of bodies fired to their maturing temperatures can be checked by observing color, hardness, porosity, sound when tapped, and degree of deformity. The samples on the bats reproduced here are bisque-fired clay at their maturing temperature.
A. Stoneware and porcelain.
B. Stoneware and grog.
C. Ferruginous and earthenware clay.

MIXTURE	underfired	mature	overfired
color	normal to pale	normal	normal to dark
irregularities	none	none	warped, collaspsed or melted
hardness	scratchable	difficult to scratch	very hard, does not scratch
porosity	very porous	porous	not very porous, or vitrified
sound	wooden	healthy sound	crystalline

Porosity

Low-firing clays (900–1050°C/1652–1922°F) are porous; stoneware (1150–1300°C/2102–2372°F) and porcelain (firing at 1250–1360°C/2282–2480°F) are considered nonporous because of their low capacity to absorb water. Clays absorbing less than 1 percent water are called vitrified.

The porosity of a piece of clay can be checked using the following method:
1. Weigh a sample that has been bisque-fired to its temperature of maturity.
2. Soak the sample 12 hours in room temperature water, or 2 hours in boiling water.
3. Remove the sample and let the water drain off.
4. Weigh it again.

The absorption capacity is calculated thus:

$$\frac{\text{damp weight} - \text{dry weight x } 100}{\text{dry weight}} = \text{absorption}$$

For example, if the weight of a dry bisque-fired piece of clay is 162 g and its damp weight is 165 g, applying the above formula yields:

$$\frac{165 - 162 \times 100}{162} = \frac{3 \times 100}{162} = \frac{300}{162} = 1.85 \text{ \% absorption}$$

Thus porosity is the water absorption capacity of a ceramic body that has been bisque-fired to its temperature of maturity.

HAND-BUILDING TOOLS

Canvas or sacking. Since the clay does not stick to this material, it is useful when forming slabs or strips of clay.

Wooden slats. Slats come in different thicknesses and are used in pairs, in conjunction with a rolling pin and canvas. They are indispensable for preparing slabs or strips of particular thicknesses.

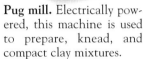

Scrapers. A useful tool, the serrated-edge scraper is used to cut slabs and strips of clay and to smooth surfaces or add texture. The angled metal blades are attached to a handle. It is helpful to have several scrapers with different-sized cutting ends, about 2 to 3.5 cm (^{3}/4–1^1/4 in.) or even wider.

Pug mill. Electrically powered, this machine is used to prepare, knead, and compact clay mixtures.

Spatulas and ribs. Generally made of wood but also available in plastic or other materials, these are fundamental for hand-building. These tools come in a wide range of shaped ends to allow for a variety of functions.

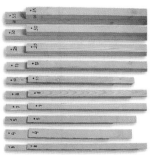

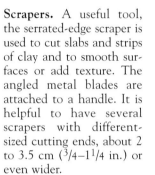

Rolling pins. Made of hard polished wood, rolling pins are used to prepare slabs and strips of clay. It is helpful to have several different sizes on hand.

Slab roller. This simple machine produces slabs of clay. It has two rollers, one fixed and the other adjustable, between which the clay is squeezed. It serves the same purpose as the rolling pin and wooden slats.

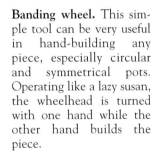
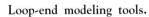

Banding wheel. This simple tool can be very useful in hand-building any piece, especially circular and symmetrical pots. Operating like a lazy susan, the wheelhead is turned with one hand while the other hand builds the piece.

Loop-end modeling tools. These are used to hollow out solid pieces, as well as to smooth off surfaces. The handle (generally made of wood) supports a metal loops of varying shape. Rounded loops are used to remove excess clay; angular hoops are used to smooth surfaces, such as the flat bottom of a pot.

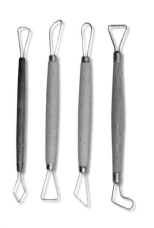

PINCH POTS
BUILDING A BOWL

*T*o make a bowl with this method, take a kneaded ball of clay (in this case stoneware) in one hand and push the thumb of the other hand into it. Pinch the ball between thumb and index fingers and rotate it to open it, pulling the walls upward and outward until the desired shape is attained.

1. Make a ball from a piece of stoneware and hold it loosely in the palm of the hand. Cup the other hand and pat the ball gently.

2. Once the ball is ready, wet your right thumb to help push it into the ball.

3. Push your thumb into the ball of clay.

4. Wet your thumb again, place it in the hole just made, and pinch the clay between index finger and thumb to open the hole more.

5. Continue to pinch the ball while turning it to widen the hole; push upward and outward to raise the walls.

1

2

3

4

5

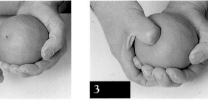

6

6. Continuing with the same process, enlarge the bowl and thin the walls. Be sure your thumb is wet to prevent cracking the walls.

7. The bowl is now shaped. Even out the thickness of the rim with your index fingers.

8. Three bowls made with the pinch method. I have left the rims irregular but have tried to even out the thickness of the walls. I make the base for bowls like these by holding the bowl with my thumb and middle finger and striking it gently against the table.

9. The glazed bowls.

Joaquim Chavarria.
Bowls I, II, III, 1997
7 x 11, 5 x 10, 4 x 9 (2³/₄ x 4³/₈, 2 x 4, 1⁵/₈ x 3¹/₂ in.).
Firing temperature: 1250°C (2282°F).

7

8

9

BUILDING A VASE

*I*n the previous exercise I began with a ball of clay. In this one I will use small lumps of red earthenware, which I will press together piece by piece with my thumbs and index fingers, slowly forming the walls by pulling upward and making sure they are uniform. I will form a circular shape by sticking the pieces of clay together bit by bit until the vase is complete. Although this method is very quick, it is necessary to stop from time to time to allow the walls to harden somewhat or they will collapse under the weight. To do this, cover the upper part with a piece of plastic wrap for a time.

Because the pinch method produces very solid walls, this technique can be used for large pots.

1. First make the base of the vase. Knead a lump of clay, striking it with the base of your palm and then with the side of your hand, attempting to maintain a uniform thickness. Lift the slab of clay thus formed in both hands and let it fall onto a piece of canvas to achieve the right thickness; the impact makes it spread out in all directions. Repeat the operation several times until the correct thickness of about 1 cm (3/8 in.) is reached.

2. Cut the lump of clay with a metal cutter, scraper, or knife. With a potter's needle score the part of the base where you will stick the first strip to begin the walls.

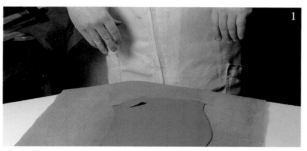

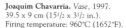

3. If you don't have clay powder on hand to prepare slip, use this emergency procedure. Hand-build a small bowl using the pinch method and pour some water in it. Stirring the water causes some clay from the walls to mix into the water, thus forming slip, which can be applied to the scored area with a paintbrush.

4. Prepare a small strip of clay from the part left over from cutting the base and place it over the scored area of the base.

5. With the potter's needle score the lower edge and the interior of the strip and place a coil of clay on it to aid in joining. Smooth the join with a wooden modeling tool.

6. Begin hand-building using the pinching technique. Overlap a small lump of clay onto the strip, pressing with your thumb and index fingers and pulling upward to keep the walls from sagging. Rotate the base, continuing to add small lumps until the circle is complete.

7. Raise the wall using four layers of pinched clay. Strengthen the joins in the interior of the piece, then smooth them with the wooden modeling tool while holding the outside of the wall with your left hand to keep it from deforming. Do not smooth the joins on the outside of the wall; leave them visible. Cover the rim with a sheet of plastic and allow the lower part to dry for an hour.

8 and **9.** Continue to add pieces of clay in the same way, stopping twice more during the process to allow the walls to harden. The photo shows the piece before and after glazing and firing.

Joaquim Chavarria. *Vase*, 1997.
39.5 x 9 cm (15 1/2 x 3 1/2 in.).
Firing temperature: 960°C (1652°F).

ZOOMORPHIC PIECE

I began this exercise (using stoneware with fine grog) with the intention of making a vase with two spouts and three supporting conical feet. During the hand-building process, my original idea changed as I saw that the shape of the piece suggested an animal form. The two spouts became the necks and heads of a two-headed creature; the three support feet became four legs. Gradually it was transformed into a zoomorphic shape.

Such a change in ideas in the middle of the hand-building process is not unusual and can be positive. Any idea should be flexible enough to be changed during hand-building.

1. Build the base from small pieces of stoneware clay mixed with grog, using the pinch method so the pieces overlap and attempting to maintain the same thickness. Smooth the surface off with the fingers before adding the wall.

2. Build the base of the walls by overlapping small pieces of clay, added while rotating the base. Continue with the second row, adding the bits of clay from the inside by pressing with your index fingers from the inside and your thumbs from the outside until each bit of clay is joined to the previous one in the row and to the lower one. Attempt to maintain an even wall thickness as you shape it.

3. When you have finished adding the first two or three rows, smooth off and unify the inside with the rounded end of a wooden modeling tool. If working with vases or pots that have straight walls, you can use the squared end of the modeling tool.

4. Using a wooden slat, pat the outer surface to compact and shape it. To prevent deformations, use the other hand to support the wall from the inside.

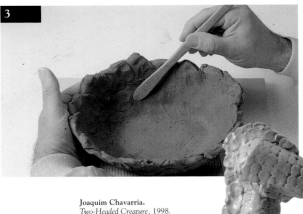

Joaquim Chavarria.
Two-Headed Creature, 1998.
36 x 28 x 18 cm (14¹⁄₈ x 11 x 7¹⁄₈ in.).

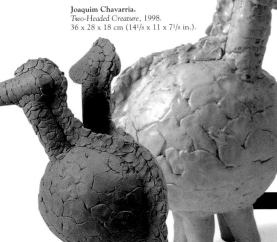

5. From three strips of cardboard joined with adhesive tape, make an arch to serve as reinforcement so you can close the sphere without waiting for the clay to harden.

6. View of the sphere before it is closed, with the cardboard reinforcement acting like the arches in a Gothic ceiling.

7. Begin to build one of the cylindrical necks. Use the wooden modeling tool to unify the interior, and then begin with the second neck. Cover the top of the necks with a piece of plastic to keep in the moisture, allowing the lower part of the necks to dry and become harder before adding the heads.

8. Build the heads and stick them in place with slip. Then make the legs, which are hollow truncated cones. Allow them to dry before sticking them to the animal's belly. Before attaching the last leg, make a small ventilation hole in the belly and the leg, and place the leg so it covers the hole, thus allowing air to reach the inside. To finish off the piece, apply small pieces of clay along the back to form a ridge and add a tail.

9. View of the finished piece.

SPHERICAL VASE

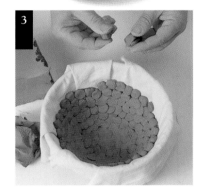

T his exercise presents a slight variation on the pinch technique. Using small balls of stoneware with fine grog, I line the inside of a plastic bowl that will act as a mold. I will also need a metal cake ring (a ring of cardboard will also work) and a cup.

1. Begin with clay, a bowl, and a clean cotton cloth.

2. Prepare several small balls of the clay. Cover the bowl with the cloth to keep the clay from sticking. Pinch the balls and press them around the inside of the bowl.

3. Prepare the balls as you work; they will dry out if you prepare too many at once.

4. With your right index finger, smooth off and unify the inner surface of the wall. When you reach the top, hold the upper row in place with your left thumb while smoothing it.

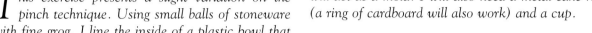

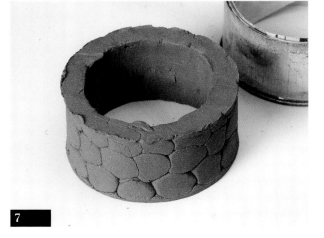

5. While the piece is drying, begin making the ring that will form the base. Cover the inner surface of a metal cake ring or a cardboard cylinder with paper towels, which serve the same purpose as the cloth. Line the inner surface of the ring with small balls of clay in the same manner as before.

6. After all the balls are in place and the ring is covered in clay, smooth the inner surface with a wooden modeling tool.

7. View of the finished base.

8. After building the base, remove the clay lining the bowl, which should now be sufficiently hard. Prepare another bowl of clay the same way. When you finish, measure the circumference with a string, or calculate it with the arithmetic formula: $L = 2\pi r$ (where r is the radius and $\pi = 3.1416$).

9. If you used the string method, measure the string to determine the length.

10. Place two slats each 7 mm ($^1/4$ in.) thick on a canvas. To keep them separated place between them two wooden blocks each 3 cm ($1^1/8$ in.) wide. Fill the space between the slats with freshly prepared small balls of clay to cover an area corresponding to the length of the circumference. Hold the slats in place with your other hand as you work.

11. Smooth out the strip of clay with a scraper. This strip will serve to unite the two halves of the sphere.

12. While the strip hardens a bit, begin to prepare the neck of the vase. To achieve the truncated cone shape, use a plaster cup as a mold, or a glass cup covered with paper towels. Proceed in the same fashion.

13. View of the neck mold, upside down, covered in small balls of clay.

14. View of the five parts composing the vase.

15. Score the area of contact of the two hemispheres with a potter's needle and add slip.

16. Put the two halves together. The slip should help them stick together. Score the area along the join where the strip is to be placed and add more slip.

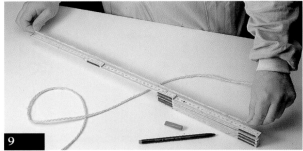

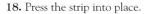

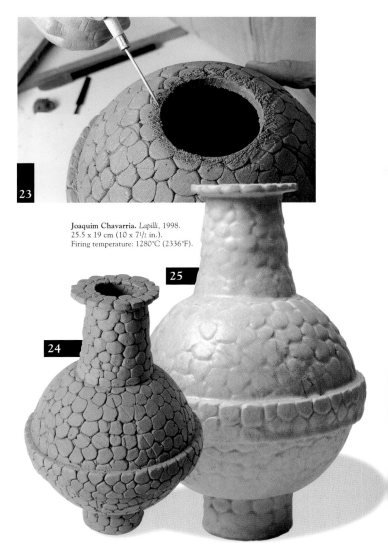

17. Place eight kiln supports or similar blocks around the spherical body of the vase to hold up the strip that will go around the circumference. Score the inner surface of the strip, spread it with slip, and place it along the join of the two bowls.

18. Press the strip into place.

19. Mark the ring where the base is to be joined to the body. Score and add slip to all the points of contact and then add the base.

20. View of the base in its place.

21. To reinforce the join, add a thin coil of clay to the inner join and smooth it with a wooden modeling tool.

22. Mark the area where the neck is to be. With a metal modeling tool, cut a hole in the sphere at this area. The cut should be made at an angle so that the piece of clay does not fall into the vase.

23. Score the areas to be joined and follow the joining procedure.

24 and **25.** Two views of the finished piece.

Joaquim Chavarria. *Lapilli,* 1998.
25.5 x 19 cm (10 x 7¹/₂ in.).
Firing temperature: 1280°C (2336°F).

BUILDING WITH COILS
CYLINDRICAL VASE

This technique allows you to build any type of pot, as long as the coils are of uniform thickness. For a piece with thick walls, the coils must also be thick; if the walls are to be thin, the coils will be thin as well. The coils are made from balls of kneaded clay. At first, you should not make the coils too long, only up to about 25 cm (10 in.) in length. The longer they are, *the harder it is to maintain a uniform thickness in the coils. With practice it will become easier.*

Before beginning, calculate the quantity of coils necessary for the piece to be modeled. Prepare them and place them on a piece of plastic or a wet rag that has been wrung out so they keep their moisture and don't dry out before you use them.

1. Prepare various balls of red earthenware, building them with the palms of your hands.

2. Place the balls on a piece of plastic. Begin making a coil by rolling a ball on the table to thin it, using the fingertips of one hand.

3. With both hands and a back and forth movement, continue to thin and elongate the clay. Note how the thumbs are crossed to help steady the hands.

4. With hands in the same position and same movement, move them along the coil (without pressing down) to obtain desired length.

5. Once the coils are prepared, make a spiral with one of them for the base of the cylindrical vase.

6. With a wooden modeling tool, join the parts of the spiral by smoothing the surface of both sides from the outer edge toward the center.

7. Smooth off the surface of the base with a scraper. With a potter's needle, score the area where the first coil is to be placed.

8. Paint the scored area with slip and score the first coil.

9. Place the first coil on the base, making sure that its length is equal to or greater than the circumference of the base.

10. With the scraper, cut off any extra length of coil at an angle. This makes the surface of contact between the ends of the coils larger than if the cut were done perpendicularly.

11. With a rounded modeling tool, join the coils on the inside of the vase.

12. Once the inside is smoothed, smooth the outside in the same way.

13. With a serrated scraper, unify the outer wall and make sure it is vertical.

14. Continue to add coils. To avoid cracks during the drying stage, make sure the points where the two ends of each coil join do not coincide vertically with the ends of other coils. You can see that the second coil was too short, so I added a piece to it.

15. With the diagonal edge of the serrated scraper, bevel the outer edge of the base. Once the coils are all in place, go over them with the serrated edge of the scraper. Let the finished pot dry.

16. View of the vase once glazed.

Joaquim Chavarria.
Cylinder, 1997.
15 x 8 cm (5⁷/8 x 3¹/8 in.).
Firing temperature: 960°C

ORGANIC PIECE

This exercise utilizes an asymmetrical shape with some of the coils left visible to enhance the volume of the piece. As you will see when you make this piece, the coils mold themselves perfectly to the shapes you choose for the vase, thus the method can be adapted to almost any piece. While you are working on the upper part, the lower part is drying.

1. Prepare a number of coils made of stoneware with medium grog and place them on a piece of plastic. In the photo I am building a longer coil for the base.

2. Make a spiral to form the base and attach several more coils to enlarge it. Attach the coils well so the structure is sturdy.

3. View of the finished base.

4. With the potter's needle, lute the joins on both sides of the base.

5. Using the wooden modeling tool with a rounded edge, smooth and compact the joins to give them more strength.

6. Finish smoothing off both surfaces with the scraper.

7. Score the area of the base where the first coil is to be added.

8. After painting the area with slip, add the first row of coils. This portion can be made of one or several coils.

9. Cut the ends of the coils diagonally to provide a greater surface of contact. The first coil should be well placed, following the contours of the base perfectly.

10. Place a coil inside, along the join between the first coil and base to reinforce it.

11. Add more coils, raising the walls and making them wider by placing each coil toward the outer edge of the one below. Smooth the inner wall with the wooden modeling tool. This closeup shows the outer surface and the smoothed inner wall.

12. Smooth out the outer wall and continue to add coils unevenly.

13. With a serrated scraper, smooth off the outer wall. This part can now dry while the rest is made.

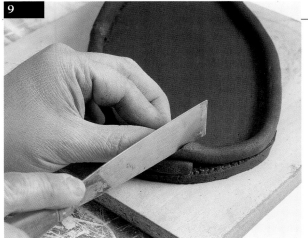

14. In the second phase, score the rim of the finished part of the vase where the next coil will be placed.

15. After adding slip to the scored area, place the next scored coil on the vase.

16. Here I am placing a coil along the outer join of the two top coils. Hold the coil with your left hand while pressing it in place with your right index finger. At the same time, use your right thumb to keep the upper coil from moving.

17. The piece continues to grow in all directions. Add parts of coils to make elevations over which the visible coils will flow. From this point on, the vase will begin to close.

18. After joining the previous coils, begin to add the coils that are to remain visible.

19. Here I am adding the sixth visible coil. With the index finger and thumb of your left hand press this coil in place while you hold and align it from underneath with your middle finger. Note how the coils hold up and begin to form a cupola. With each additional coil, add an extra, smaller one along the join on the inside, unifying the inner wall.

20. After luting and adding the unifying coils, go over the upper surface with a metal modeling tool.

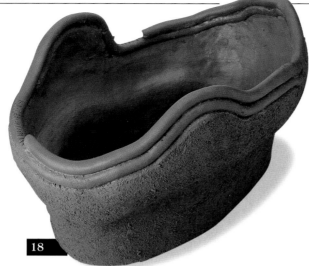

21. To achieve the desired form, build the coils with your fingers as you go along.

22. In the third phase, build the neck of the vase. Note that I finish each added part as I go along. I have again left some coils visible. In this picture I am adding a coil inside the neck to reinforce the larger outer coils.

23–25. Finish the neck with smoothed coils. Different views of the finished piece.

Joaquim Chavarria.
Organic Piece, 1998.
37.5 x 26.5 x 20 cm
(14⅞ x 10⅜ x 7⅞ in.).
Firing temperature: 1280°C
(2336°F).

RECTANGULAR BOTTLE

*F*or this rectangular bottle, the placing of the coils differs somewhat from the method used in the previous example. Interspersed among the structural coils are others that give the impression of fragility. This is just an illusion, since, as you will see during the hand-building process, all the coils are perfectly joined and reinforced with extra coils and smoothed off on the interior.

1. For this piece I used stoneware with fine grog. Form some balls from which to make coils, which will be used to build the bottle.

2. Make a rectangular spiral with one of the coils to form the base. Using a wooden modeling tool, unify the coils, with strokes moving inward from the outer edge of the circle. Smooth off the surface.

3. With a potter's needle, score the area where the first coil of the wall is to be placed. Add slip before adding the coil to make sure it is well joined.

4. As you add coils, also place thinner, reinforcing coils in the inside along the joins. Smooth them with the squared edge of the modeling tool, unifying the inner wall.

5. With the aid of two pieces of wood connected at a 90° angle, add some cut coils, placed vertically, and add thinner coils along the inner joins, as before.

6. After building this frieze, add three horizontal coils and then a row of spirals symmetrically alternating in direction. Then add another three horizontal coils and another row of vertical pieces, finishing off the body with three more horizontal coils.

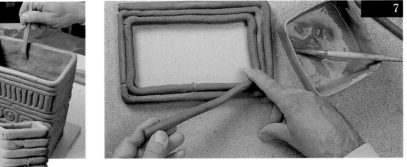

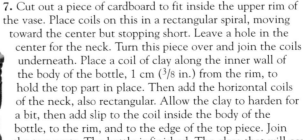

7. Cut out a piece of cardboard to fit inside the upper rim of the vase. Place coils on this in a rectangular spiral, moving toward the center but stopping short. Leave a hole in the center for the neck. Turn this piece over and join the coils underneath. Place a coil of clay along the inner wall of the body of the bottle, 1 cm (³/8 in.) from the rim, to hold the top part in place. Then add the horizontal coils of the neck, also rectangular. Allow the clay to harden for a bit, then add slip to the coil inside the body of the bottle, to the rim, and to the edge of the top piece. Join the two parts. The bottle is finished. The glaze that will cover the interior will further reinforce the piece.

8. View of the finished bottle during drying.

9. View of the bottle after glazing and firing.

Joaquim Chavarria. *Colombina*, 1998.
37 x 19 x 13 cm (14⁵/8 x 7¹/2 x 5¹/8 in.).
Firing temperature: 1260°C (2300°F).

OPEN CYLINDRICAL VASE

*T*his exercise uses a stoneware mixture with fine grog. It is a variation of the conventional method of handbuilding with coils. In the previous pieces, the coils were joined together forming a compact wall. Here they will only intersect at some small points of contact. It is delicate work because of the fragility of the coils. But after the bisque-firing stage the piece will be strong enough to be handled without problems.

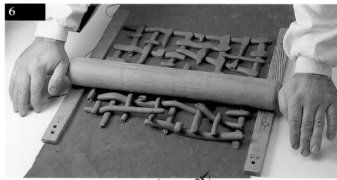

4. Wrap the cardboard tube in newspaper, tape it in place, and measure the circumference of the tube with a string.

5. Interlace the coils on a piece of canvas, covering an area equal in width to the circumference of the cardboard tube and in length to the approximate height of the tube.

6. Without touching the coils, place a wooden slats 10 mm (³/8 in.) thick on each side and flatten the coils to that thickness with a rolling pin. This joins the coils at their intersections.

7. The pressure of the rolling pin forms the overlapping coils into a unified mesh. Place the tube over the coils so that their width matches that of the tube.

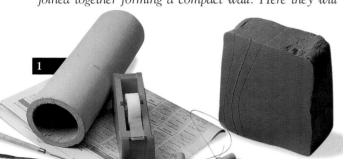

1. Here are the materials: stoneware with grog, modeling tools, scraper, potter's needle, cutting wire, adhesive tape, a cardboard tube for support, and newspaper. You'll also need a string for measuring and a piece of canvas.

2. Calculate the approximate number of coils needed and make the balls from which to build them.

3. Form the coils about 15 mm (⁵/8 in.) thick.

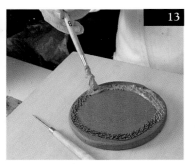

14. Score the part of the coils that will come into contact with the base and add slip.

15. Place the cylinder back on the base, on the scored area, and press gently to join the two parts. Lute the joins with the needle and reinforce it with a thin coil.

16. Put your hand in the upper part of the tube and carefully pull upward to remove it, leaving the newspaper behind to act as a support for the clay until it hardens some more. The newspaper does not prevent the piece from shrinking or drying quickly.

17. Remove the newspaper after three hours, by which time the piece will be hard enough to handle. View of the finished piece.

18. View of the piece after firing.

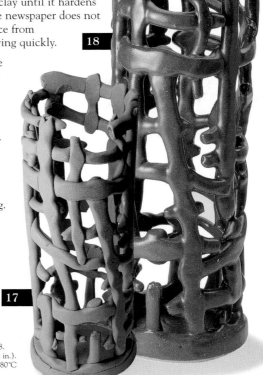

8. Lift the canvas with the meshed coils and roll them onto the tube until they cover its full circumference.

9. Once this is accomplished, you will have a cylinder covering the tube. Stand it up and let harden for an hour.

10. Build the base out of two coils placed in spiral form.

11. Using a wooden modeling tool, unify the coils on both sides of the base, with strokes moving inward from the outer edge of the circle.

12. Place the cylinder with the tube on the base and mark the perimeter with a potter's needle.

13. Remove the cylinder. Score the contact areas of the base with the needle and paint them with slip.

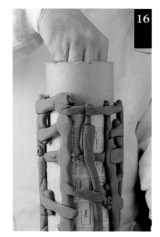

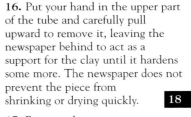

Joaquim Chavarria.
Eulogy to Space IX, 1998.
32 x 11 cm (12⅝ x 4⅜ in.).
Firing temperature: 1280°C
(2336°F).

BUILDING WITH STRIPS
VASE WITH HANDLES

*T*his technique is similar to the slab-building method, since it begins with a slab that is subsequently cut into strips. The strips must be narrow, 3 cm (1¹/8 in.) at most, especially if they are to be used to make pieces with round bases. The width of the strips will depend on the shape of the piece. Before starting to build, all the strips should be prepared and covered so that they do not dry out. Use slip to strengthen the joins, which should also be luted with a potter's needle and reinforced with coils.

The strip-building method can be used to create many different types of ceramic pieces, including bowls, goblets, vases, plates, and sculptures. This exercise uses red earthenware to build a vase.

1. Prepare some coils with a diameter of 2 cm (³/4 in.) by working the clay with both hands to shape it. These coils will be used to make the slab and are not the same as those used in the previous exercises for building with the coil method.

2. Place the coils next to each other on a piece of canvas and press them together with your thumbs.

3. Widen the surface of the slab by adding more coils and following the same process.

4. Place a wooden slat 8 mm (⁵/16 in.) thick on each side of the slab. Using a rolling pin, gently move back and forth over the slab to flatten it. Note that a small space should be left between the slats and the slab to prevent the clay from rising onto the slats as you flatten it.

5. During the rolling process, stop periodically and lift the slab off the canvas to prevent it from sticking and not stretching. View of the finished 8 mm (⁵/16 in.) slab.

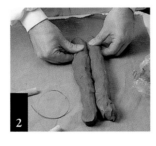

6. Using a wooden slat 3 mm (¹/8 in.) wide as a guide, measure off and cut the necessary strips (at least 15) with a scraper.

7. Place the strips as shown around the base. Bend eight strips in a horseshoe shape to use to widen the body of the vase and then make it more narrow. Note that they are bent to follow the circumference of the base and that each one fits into the next.

8. Place a melamine-coated board on a banding wheel and put the base on it. With a potter's needle, score the area where the first strip is to be placed and add slip.

9. Score the lower edge of the first strip to be placed on the base.

10. Place the first strip on the base, making sure it is correctly positioned. Be certain to place it on top of the base and not around the outside edge, so that the strip will open outward as desired, not lean inward.

11. Once the strip is in place, cut the extra part diagonally. Score and add slip to the two ends of the strip and stick them together. Use the needle to lute all of the joins, beginning with the inside.

12. Put a coil of clay along the inside join.

13. With the wooden modeling tool, press the coil in place and smooth it, joining the first strip to the base. Do the same with the outside join and then score the upper part of the strip.

14. Continue the process by adding another strip on top of the first. With your left hand steady the strip from the outside, and control the top edge with your index finger as you lute the join between the two strips. Also score and add slip to the area of contact of the new strip.

15. View of the hand-building process with the third strip in place, which doesn't reach all the way around. Note that neither the inner nor the outer joins are visible and the surface of the wall is smooth.

16. View of the piece with four strips in place. You can see how the strips do not meet along the same vertical line, which will prevent the vase from cracking during the drying process.

17. Another view, this time with five strips, with the joins and luting visible and a coil smoothed into a central join. Although the walls should be smoothed strip by strip, the piece is shown here with all the joins visible to illustrate the process more fully.

18. Smooth over the surface of the vase with a serrated scraper to unify it.

19. Begin to close the body of the vase. To do this, place the next strip along the outside of the previous one. Lute the inner join and smooth it.

20. Continue to place strips to close the piece. After putting each strip in place, lute the inner join and smooth the wall.

21. Detail of the first short strip that will form the cylindrical neck. It rests on the inner edge of the last strip, but can also be placed on the upper surface of the last strip. Score it and smooth it in place as with the previous strips.

22. After luting and adding the reinforcing coils along the joins, finish adding the last strips of the neck. Lute the joins from both the inside and the outside and then smooth the entire vase with the serrated scraper.

23. Use a level to be sure the neck is straight.

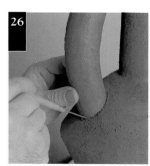

24. Continuing with the same system as with the neck, build two thinner cylinders for the handles. After they are modeled, insert a rubber tube into each and bend them carefully until they are the proper shape.

25–26. Details of the scored area where one of the handles will be attached and of the luted join of the handle with the body of the vase.

27. Once the first handle is in place, attach the second one. If part of a handle is missing, build it from a leftover piece of a strip.

28. The handles are now in place. Smooth over the surface with the serrated scraper.

29. View of the completed vase when fired.

Joaquim Chavarria. *Hands on Hips,* 1998.
43 x 21 cm (16⁷/₈ x 8¹/₈ in.).
Firing temperature: 980°C (1796°F).

RECTANGULAR VASE

*T*his exercise—one of the simplest that can be done with ceramics—requires both strips and slabs of clay, although the size of the pieces required means that more of the former will be needed. The volume of the piece is created with the strips, which results in the best possible support because of the overlaying method of the joining the strips with slip. The inner support is four strips of melamine board wrapped in newspaper. The ceramic body used for this exercise is stoneware.

1. Prepare several striplike slabs 8 mm (5/16 in.) thick, allowing the natural texture to remain once the clay has been gone over with a rolling pin.

2. Place a sheet of paper on the melamine board to prevent the clay from sticking to it, then place the base strip on the board. Set the support column over the center of the base.

3. Make cuts in four places of the base so it can be folded it in four parts without breaking.

4. Score the joint and join it with slip.

5. Fold the lateral strips of the vase over the others and pat them with a flat piece of wood until they are well adhered.

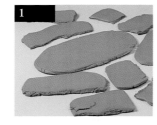

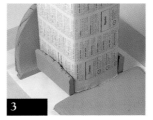

6. Place the first strip within the space left by the four lateral strips and then overlap the next one; continue in this manner.

7. This strip has been stuck to the others by applying slip and pressing over it with the piece of wood. First work on the laterals and then the central ones until the piece is completed.

8. Remove the support by carefully pulling out one strip of wood at a time. Leave the newspaper inside until the piece has hardened a little.

9. Remove the newspaper and the vase is finished. This technique makes it unnecessary to lute the interior, since the strips have been adequately stuck together.

10. This is what the vase looks like after glazing.

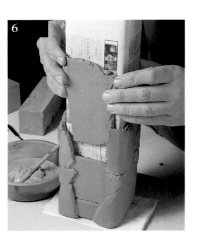

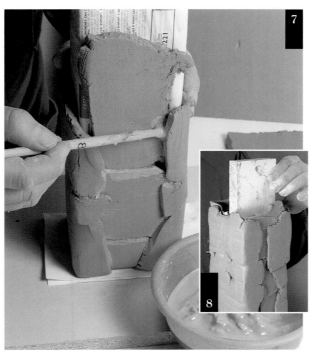

Joaquim Chavarria. *Vase for Branches*, 1998.47 x 9 cm x 8.5 cm (18¹/₂ x 3¹/₂ x 3¹/₄ in.).Firing temperature: 1250°C (2282°F).

CUP

This cup is made with strips, which undulate on one side of the stand, while the other is cut straight. In the concavity of the cup both sides will remain uncut; the coils are flattened with a rolling pin. The piece is made from stoneware with grog.

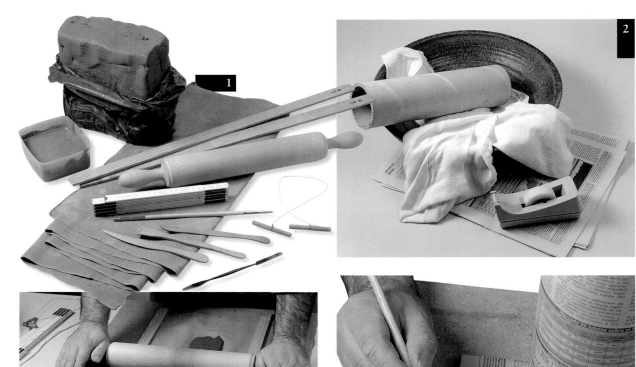

1. Here are the supplies needed: stoneware with grog body, slip, canvas, rolling pin, cutting wire, and wooden and metal ribs.

2. Also needed are a container to use as a mold (here, a ceramic bowl), some clean rags, a cardboard tube, adhesive tape, and newspaper. Cover the tube with two sheets of newspaper fastened with the tape.

3. Begin by preparing the strips that will be used to make the stand of the cup.

4. Cut each strip down the middle to form two pieces. Cut one of the sides straight, which will be covered by overlap. Cut the other side unevenly.

5. Place the base on the worksurface and on top of it place the covered tube. Score the area jutting out beyond the tube.

6. Choose the first strip and score the area of contact with the base using the potter's needle. Apply slip and place it over the tube, pressing down on it.

7. Once the first strip has been placed, attach it to the base by luting and placing the coil over the joint.

8. Smooth down the coil that reinforces the joint. The first strip is finished.

9. Score the top of the first strip, the zone of contact with the second strip, and the sinuous surface of the interior of the second strip.

10. Apply slip over these areas.

11. Place the second strip on top of the first so are properly aligned. Press them firmly together, making sure not to distort the vase.

12. Prepare more strips to apply using the same technique.

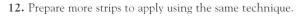

13. Stick down the fourth strip around the tube. Note the abundant slip and scoring.

14. Eight strips have now been adhered. The stand of the cup begins to emerge, looking like an inverted palm tree trunk.

15. At strip number eight, cut the surplus clay with a metal rib. Use the top of the tube as a reference so the strips form a uniform shape.

17

19

20

16

16. View of the finished stand.

17. Prepare the strips and base for bowl portion. Parts of the strips have been curved so that they can be overlapped, so that one part will be inside the piece while the other side will remain visible on the exterior part of the cup.

18. Line the ceramic bowl with rags so the base will not stick to the strips.

19. Bend the strips carefully into the shape of a horseshoe, so that they gradually form the shape of the bowl. Two strips are needed here to cover the bowl's circumference.

20. Once the base of the cup has been formed, score the area of contact. Note the circular shape of the base and the irregular cut for the look I want for this piece.

21. Spread slip over the scored zone.

22. Place the first strip on the base. This strip has already been scored and spread with slip.

23. Using a sponge, press down firmly over the joint, shaping it to the form of the bowl.

21

22

23

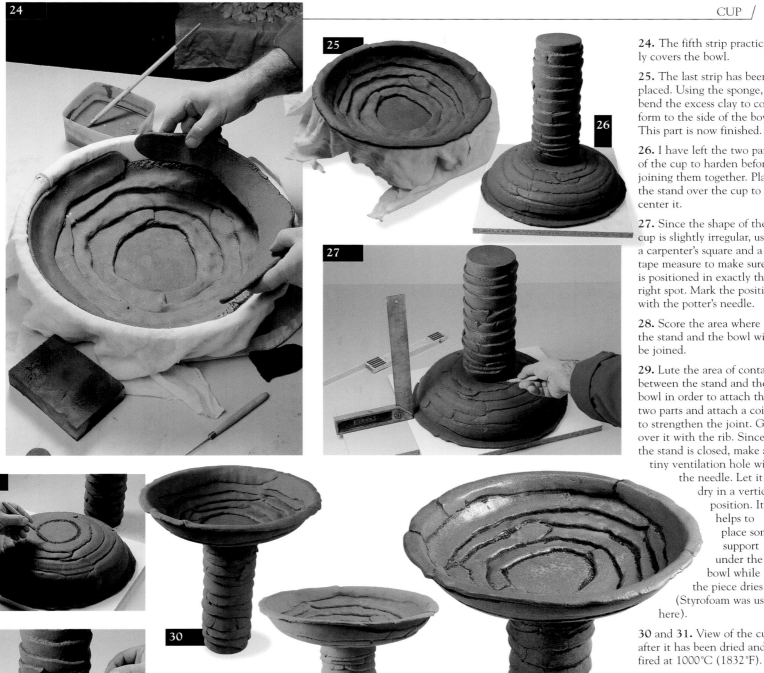

24. The fifth strip practically covers the bowl.

25. The last strip has been placed. Using the sponge, bend the excess clay to conform to the side of the bowl. This part is now finished.

26. I have left the two parts of the cup to harden before joining them together. Place the stand over the cup to center it.

27. Since the shape of the cup is slightly irregular, use a carpenter's square and a tape measure to make sure it is positioned in exactly the right spot. Mark the position with the potter's needle.

28. Score the area where the stand and the bowl will be joined.

29. Lute the area of contact between the stand and the bowl in order to attach the two parts and attach a coil to strengthen the joint. Go over it with the rib. Since the stand is closed, make a tiny ventilation hole with the needle. Let it dry in a vertical position. It helps to place some support under the bowl while the piece dries (Styrofoam was used here).

30 and **31.** View of the cup after it has been dried and fired at 1000°C (1832°F).

32. The glazed cup.

Joaquim Chavarria. *Cup*, 1998. 34 x 34 cm (13³/s x 13³/s in.). Firing temperature: 1280°C (2336°F).

GEOMETRIC CONSTRUCTION

Ceramics made with strips must be planned carefully. Before beginning, prepare the ceramic body needed to make the slabs from which the strips will be cut. The previous exercises used damp strips; in this one the clay is leather-hard to prevent the strips from warping as the volume is formed. The piece is made from stoneware with medium-grain grog.

1. Calculate the approximate number of slabs needed to make this work and prepare them 8 mm (5/16 in.) thick. Leave the slabs overnight to harden.

2. Using a scraper and a set square used as a guide, cut out a rectangular slab to form the base. Cover the remaining slabs in plastic to prevent them from drying out.

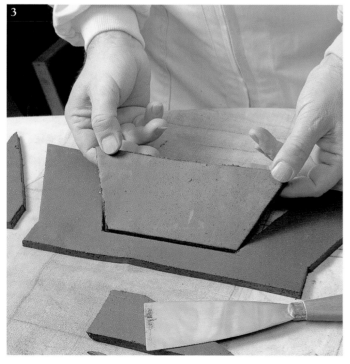

3. Prepare the two main slabs that will be placed over the base. Cut along their inner part.

4. Place one of the slabs over the base, situated on the work surface, and with a needle mark the line indicating the area where the two pieces will be joined together.

5. Using the potter's needle, score the area and spread slip over it.

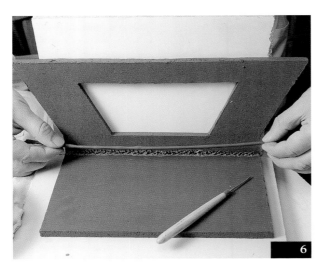

6. Position the first wall and use the set square to check that the wall is completely vertical. Lute the area and place a coil to strengthen it.

7. View of the first stage of the construction, with the two walls positioned.

8. Enclose the inner space with strips, producing a tubular volume. Pierce a ventilation hole in the base slab.

9. Score and apply slip on another slab and use it to seal off the top, as well as the faces of the other slabs.

10. View of the work at a more advanced stage, in which I have modeled the pyramidal-truncated volume. Note the ventilation holes, which will communicate with every modeled part and prevent closed zones inside the work. This practice keeps the parts from breaking during the firing process, when the heat causes the volume of air inside the piece to increase.

11. Finish up by placing a coil around the base. Pat the surface with a smooth wooden modeling tool.

12. Another view of the work. The strip of wood acts as a buffer to maintain the alignment of the part separated from the main body of the work.

13. Cut the excess clay off the slab with a scraper. Go over the joint, reinforcing the area with a coil.

14. With the scraper, go over the edge of one of the volumes, using the strip of wood as a guide.

15. Cut out four strips, two of a trapezoid shape and two rectangular. With a needle, score the area where they will be joined together. Once joined together, these strips will form a truncated pyramidal volume.

16. Apply slip to one of the sides of the rectangular strips.

17. With a slat of wood as a support, and a set square, place one of the rectangular strips over the trapezoid. Lute the joint and place a coil over it.

18. View of the three attached strips just before attaching the fourth one.

19. Continue preparing the strips needed to construct the prism that joins the two truncated-pyramids.

20. View of the work after this shape has been placed.

21. Prepare another form situated on the board with new strips. In the slab, seen in the foreground, I have used a potter's needle to draw the outline of the cover, which I will cut out using the scraper.

22. Place this form in place on the work; it is supported behind and on either side, luted, and applied with slip. The lower support holds this form in place until it can do so on its own. Note another form that is about to be placed and in which a ventilation hole has been made, which coincides with that of the lower volume. The lowermost part of this volume also has a hole.

23–26. Views of the finished and fired work.

Joaquim Chavarria. *Balance V,* 1998
52 x 37 x 23 cm (20¹/₂ x 14⁵/₈ x 9 in.).
Firing temperature: 1250°C (2282°F).

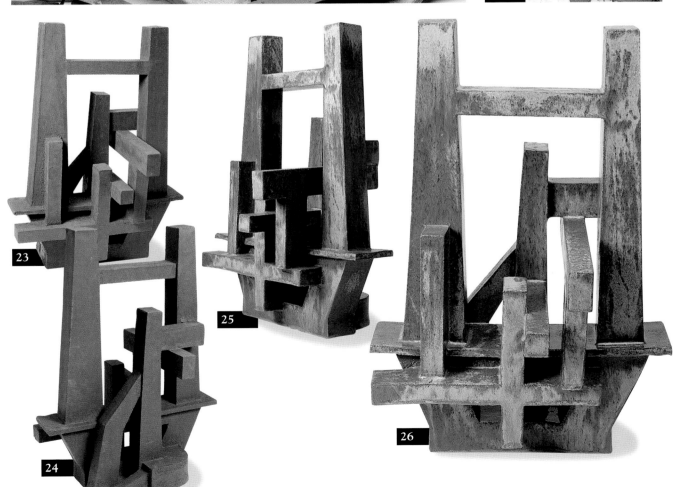

BUILDING WITH SLABS
RECTANGULAR VASE

T his exercise, carried out using stoneware with fine grog, utilizes leather-hard slabs of clay. The height of the slabs will not allow me to work with them while they are damp since they would droop over, so I prepare them in advance to be handled several hours later.

During the process of placing the slabs in position, one step may cause problems: the moment of placing the second-largest slab. Why this one and not the second-largest lateral one? I place this one first because the aperture inserted before situating the lateral one allows me to lute inside and place a joint coil in a much larger zone, which strengthens the piece. Since the lateral piece fits between the two large ones and is luted with more coils to support the exterior joint, it is safely fastened.

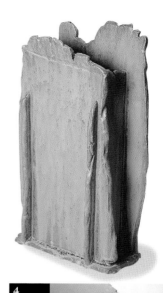

1. Prepare the coils to make the slab. Place them on a piece of canvas and press them with your thumbs to join them.

2. Along each side of the stoneware body place a slat of wood of 10 mm (3/8 in.) thick. Flatten the body with the rolling pin to form the slab.

3. Prepare three slabs: one for the base and two larger ones. Another one will be needed later, from which to create the thinner lateral slabs and the reinforcement strips.

4. With the scraper and using a metal set square as a guide, cut out the base from one of the bigger slabs. With a potter's needle, mark out a line to use as a guide for placing the lateral slabs.

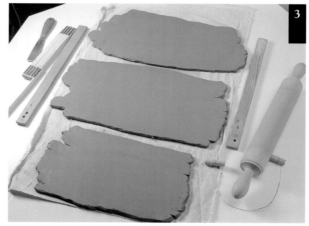

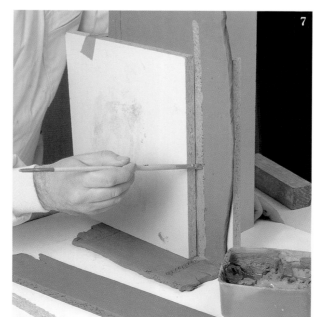

5. View of the slab with the lines marked and one edge scored, as well as the slab that will form the base, also marked out and scored on the joint of the four slabs.

6. Using two melamine boards joined with tape, prepare a set square to support the slab. In front, another board maintains the slab vertically. This board remains joined to the set square with a strip of adhesive tape (visible at the upper left).

7. In addition to maintaining the slab of stoneware, the board acts as a guide for placing the first lateral slab. Score the zone of the joint and apply slip over it. Also score part of the lateral slab (seen in the foreground).

8. Place this slab and lute all the joints of the two slabs with the potter's needle. Attach a stoneware coil to reinforce them.

9. This slabs acts as a set square and support for the largest one, thus allowing the melamine board to be removed. Press the coil against the joint with the rib. Score the area of the base where the second slab will be fitted, and apply some slip to this area and the narrow face of the lateral slab.

10. Before placing the second slab, score the joints and apply slip.

11. After placing the slab, lute the interior and attach coils to reinforce the joints. Score the narrow faces of the second lateral slab and apply slip over them and over the joints of the larger slabs.

12. Place the remaining clay from the slabs on the outer part to act as reinforcements and to give the illusion of penetrating the slabs. Lute all the joints and place coils on top to seal them.

13. Once the two supports have been placed on one of the slabs, it's time to do the same to the other slab. Mark its position and score the area where it is to be joined, continuing with the process carried out in the previous step.

14–16. View of the glazed finished piece.

Joaquim Chavarria.
Vase for Flowers, 1998.
41 x 22.5 x 11.5 cm (16^{1}/8 x 8^{3}/4 x 4^{1}/2 in.).
Firing temperature: 1250°C (2282°F).

SCULPTURAL WALL

Working with slabs sometimes requires the move-ment of large quantities of ceramic body, as seen in this exercise, which shows how to build a "wall" using a single slab. It is essential to handle the clay in a plastic state to build this piece. Stoneware with medium grog was used for this work; the grog will prevent excessive reduction during the drying time and the characteristics of the ceraminc body will produce more realistic and natural textures.

1. Prepare the coils to make the slab. Each coil must measure 5 cm (2 in.) in dia-meter for the necessary slab thickness of 3 cm (1 1/8 in.). Lay them out parallel over a piece of canvas and place a strip of wood 3 cm (1 1/8 in.) thick along each side.

2. Press the coils together with your thumbs to obtain the desired width, which will later be the height of the piece.

3. Go back and forth over the coils with a rolling pin, stretching the slab and flattening it out until the necessary length is reached.

4. Model the slab with a scraper, using the two slats of wood as a guide. One of the narrow faces of the slab will be used as the work base.

5. In order to lift up the slab without touching it with your fingers, which would leave marks, place a piece of chipboard under and over the canvas, thus making a sandwich. Place the melamine boards so that the slab is perpendicular to the floor and continue building it until you attain the desired form. Use other wooden boards to check that it is properly vertical. The 3 cm (1 1/8 in.) stoneware slab is perfectly supported without warping.

6. As you can see, I have left the faces with the coil joints visible, thus forming a natural texture. With a modeling tool you can open up spaces as windows in the wall. Use a level to ensure the verticality of the window.

7. Pierce the slab with a rectangular cake mold and with a rib make a hole wide enough to feed the cutting wire through. Allow the cutting wire to follow the outline of the cutting until the window is complete.

8. Prepare several stoneware slabs 8 mm (⁵/16 in.) thick and cut them with the rectangular cake mold. As shown, the result is similar to wooden-framed windows. Take advantage of the little squares of clay from the interior part of the wall to make the steps.

9. Fasten the little pieces inside the windows and seal them with slip. Begin to place the supports, also made of excess clay from the interior of the wall. Score the narrow faces and the parts that will be joined together with slip and stick them together. Place a coil along the joint to reinforce it.

10. Construct the steps with the little squares. Score this side of the wall as well as the area where they will be stuck and spread slip over them. Stick each step to the wall; the interior also helps to support them.

11–14. Views of both sides of the wall.

Joaquim Chavarria. *Castle Wall*, 1998.
65 x 32 x 16 cm (25⁵/8 x 12⁵/8 x 6¹/4 in.).
Firing temperature: 1280°C (2336°F).

CYLINDRICAL VASE

*T*his is the most traditional of the exercises in this chapter, in terms of the slab-building procedure. Although this work is simple, the material required for it must be handled very meticulously, both in the preparation of the slabs and in their cutting and joining. It is also important to remember that one of the sides (the one that encloses the body of the vase) will be luted and joined only on the outside, so before the base and neck are attached the part leaning on the board will

take the weight of the entire piece. I have placed a rectangular cutter in the lower end of the neck, which is thinner than the cylinder that forms the neck; to prevent it from breaking under fast-drying conditions, I have covered the entire top part (the neck and part of the body) with a piece of loose plastic sheeting to slow down the drying time. The clay used is stoneware with fine grog.

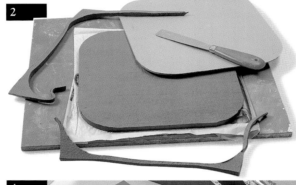

1. Prepare four slabs, about 8 mm (5/16 in.) thick; let three of them dry until they are leather-hard. The other one will be used to make the cylindrical base and neck, which should both be modeled while the clay is still elastic.

2. Cut out a cardboard template in the shape of a square with rounded corners, and place it over one of the slabs cut with a scraper. These two slabs will form two of the sides of the vase.

3. Cut out two strips from the other slab to build the other two sides of the vase.

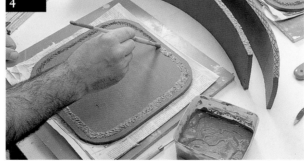

4. Using the potter's needle, score the area that will be in contact with the narrow face of the strip that will seal the piece. Also score the narrow face of the strip and apply slip to the area.

5. Place the strip on the slab, making sure that it is perpendicular to it. Use the needle to lute the area of contact. Score the two parts of the two strips and join them together with slip.

6. Place the second strip. Prepare a coil and place it over the luted interior. Join it and smooth down the area with a wooden rib.

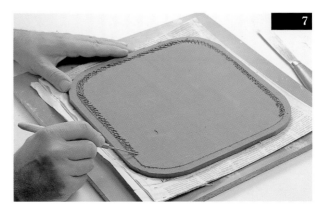

8. Seal the body of the vase with this slab. Using the wooden slat as a guide and level, check to be sure that the narrow faces of the slabs coincide vertically.

9. Cut the slab to use for building a cylinder to form the base of the vase. Keep this slab from hardening by wrapping it in a sheet of plastic. With a metal modeling tool, cut a disc over which the base cylinder will go.

10. View the base cylinder, half-formed and standing up. You can also see the cut disc.

11. Bend the strip to form the cylinder so that it coincides with the perimeter of the base. Score the joint, apply slip, and stick them together. Lute a coil and go over it with a wooden spatula. Also place a coil inside to reinforce the joint. Perforate the base so air can escape from the interior.

12. Place the cylinder base on the lateral part of the vase, mark the joint, and score both areas with the needle. Apply slip and join the two pieces, lute them, add a coil to the joint, and smooth it down. The base is now securely joined to the body of the vase. Prepare the neck in the same way as the base. Cut out the upper face of the vase and place it over the hole, sticking it down with slip and then luting the joint. Prepare a square slab to place on the mouth of the neck.

13. The piece is modeled and ready. Prepare several narrow strips 5 mm (³/16 in.) thick to place on the lateral faces. Cut each strip down the middle to obtain two strips from each piece.

14. Mark a vertical line as shown and score it with a needle. Score the narrow faces of these strips and apply slip over them, then stick them over the marked line; first the center one and then the two lateral ones. These strips, which form a little relief texture, will contrast with the vase's small walls and geometric volumes.

15 and 16. Views of the finished vase once it has been glazed.

Joaquim Chavarria. *Vase,* 1998.
57 x 24 x 10.5 cm (22¹/2 x 9¹/2 x
4¹/8 in.). Firing temperature:
1260°C (2300°F).

TROMPE L'OEIL OBJECT

*T*his exercise uses earthenware pottery, a ceramic body not commonly used for hand-building medium-sized sculptures. This body behaves perfectly on the potter's wheel but is too plastic for hand-building unless you work with small pieces. I know it will produce breakage and erosion, both in the building process and during the drying period and the firing, but I am determined to obtain the most realistic possible appearance for this subject, so I will work to overcome its drawbacks.

I also want to create contrast by using a different body for the leather straps and buckles. For them I will use red earthenware, which has the same degree of shrinkage as earthenware clay. The buckles will be covered with black engobe, prepared with iron oxide, copper, and cobalt. The finish will be a transparent matte glaze.

1. Prepare the slab from modeled coils joined together by pressing with your thumbs. Use two wooden slats each 10 mm (³/₈ in.) thick to build the slab.

2. Lay out the slab on a piece of very textured cotton fabric and place it on a cardboard tube wrapped up in newspaper.

3. Roll the slab around the tube, using the fabric in avoid touching it with your fingers, which would leave marks. With the potter's needle, score the area of contact and spread over this a layer of slip. Also score the other part of the slab that will overlap it.

4. Turn the slab over so that both parts are joined; cut the surplus piece with the scraper. Note the texture that has been printed onto the slab by the cotton fabric.

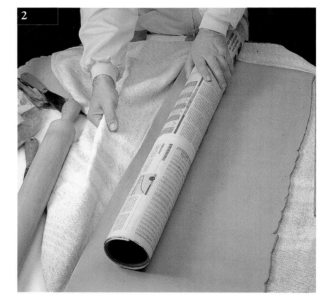

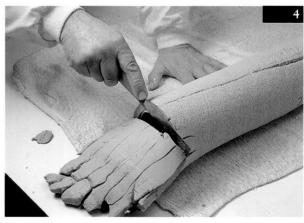

Joaquim Chavarria.
Traveling Blanket, 1998.
82 x 13 cm (32¹/₄ x 5¹/₈ in.).
Firing temperature: 960°C
(1760°F).

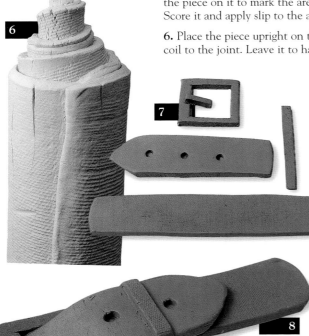

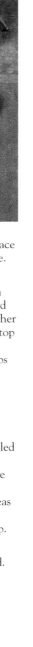

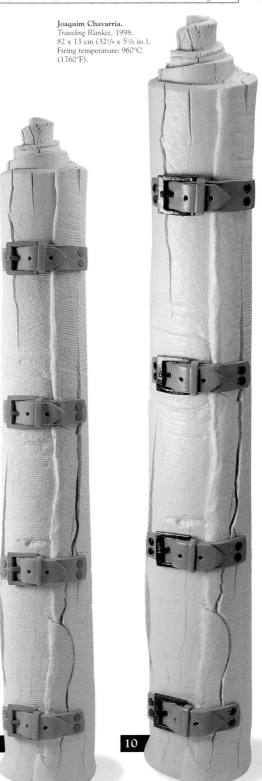

5. Prepare the other slab that will be used as a base and place the piece on it to mark the area of contact with the needle. Score it and apply slip to the area.

6. Place the piece upright on the base, lute it, and fasten a coil to the joint. Leave it to harden. Remove the cardboard tube and then roll the other slab around the tube for top part of the piece. This picture shows the tiny rips in the slab produced by applying pressure while rolling the slab up.

7. and **8.** View of the individual pieces of the straps and buckles, modeled from red earthenware. Mount them on the piece by following the usual process of scoring the areas of contact and then applying earthenware slip.

9 and **10.** Views of the work, finished and glazed.

BUILDING WITH LARGE CHUNKS OF CLAY
TEXTURED BOTTLE

This bottle starts with a chunk of stoneware clay with medium grog, worked in the state in which it comes out of the bag. This body, which is mature, has lost part of its dampness during storage and although its consistency is more akin to leather-hard clay, it is possible to build with. To conserve the textures of the body *in its natural state, I will leave the exterior in the same state as it is now. The only thing I am going to do is hollow out the chunk to make the inside of the vessel. After removing the ceramic body from the interior, I will build the neck of the bottle.*

1. Without removing it from the bag, smack the body on the table to make it more compact.

2. Remove the plastic bag, taking care not to damage the surface of the body.

3. Lay the carpenter's square over the face destined to be the base, and with the potter's needle mark out the inner rectangle within which to hollow out the piece.

4. With a looped tool, hollow out the piece, continuing until you reach the bottom. Be careful not to pierce the walls, so check the thickness at each stage with your fingers.

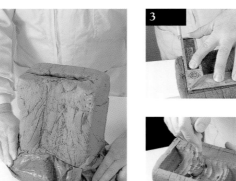

5. With a scraper, finish cutting out the aperture of the base, slanting it slightly toward the interior. This sloping rim will prevent the base from entering the hollow body of the piece.

6. Measure the rectangle of the base and prepare a slab of the same size.

7. Using the scraper and wooden slat, execute a bevel-shaped cut in the narrow faces of the slab.

8. Score all the narrow faces of this slab with the potter's needle.

9. Repeat the scoring procedure on the inner part of the mouth of the base and apply slip on top.

10. Position the base in place. Note that is also has its area of contact covered with slip.

11. View of the base sealed, luted, and with a coil placed on top to reinforce the joint. Press and smooth down the stoneware coil with a rib, leaving the base finished.

12. Use the clay removed from the chunk to make the neck of the bottle, following the same procedure used for making the body. Smack and pat it inside the plastic bag on the table.

13. Since the neck is quite tall, it will have to be cut. To do this, place a slat of wood 2 cm (³/4 in.) thick on each side and cut the clay with the cutting wire, slicing it from one corner to prevent the wire from dragging the neck with it.

14. In order to create ample contact surface, lower the base of the neck at the joint, producing a small step, and begin to hollow it out. To avoid altering the texture I decide not lute the joint; instead I will apply only slip to the joints to fasten them together. The coat of glaze applied later will reinforce the inner joint.

15. View of the hollowed-out neck now placed on top of the bottle, through which a hole was cut equal to the perimeter of the neck's rim. Score the areas of contact of the bottle's neck and body and apply slip over them.

16. Attach the neck to the vessel, pressing them together so the surplus slip seeps out.

17. Go over the joint with the needle, marking it but not luting it.

18 and **19.** Views of the finished and fired bottle.

Joaquim Chavarria.
Impression, 1998.
36 x 15 x 10 cm (14¹/8 x 5⁷/8 x 4 in.).
Firing temperature: 1280°C (2336°F).

RHINOCEROS SCULPTURE

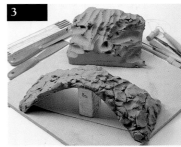

*T*he last exercise took advantage of the natural form and texture of the body to build the bottle. This one uses a more standard hand-building process: the pinching technique, which consists of superimposing little pieces of clay to make a model. This procedure is common in sculpting. When I finish the work I will hollow it out so that it dries evenly and can be bisque-fired. As the photographic sequence shows, I use a small cardboard bridge to give it its first form, and the piece quickly starts to take on the initial shape of an animal in stylized form, reinforcing the volume and leaving the natural texture produced by the pinch-building technique.

1. The materials needed for this exercise are grog fine-grain body, a cardboard template, scrapers, a metal spatula, some wooden ribs, a potter's needle, a toothed scraper, cutting wire, a looped tool, and a ruler.

2. Begin building little pieces of clay body on the cardboard support. Hold them in your left hand so they do not bend with the weight of the body.

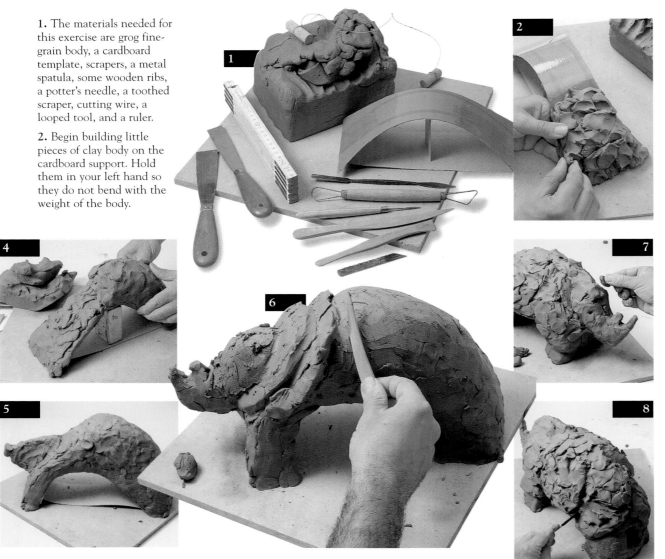

3. Because of its weight, the support should be braced underneath by a bit of wood or other material until the piece hardens enough to able to support its own weight.

4. Hold the piece under the cardboard with both hands and use your thumbs to make the clay more compact while giving it form.

5 and 6. View of the work at an advanced stage. With the rib or spatula bring out the animal's shape, in this case a rhinoceros.

7 and 8. Pinch by pinch, continue building. Note the surface treatment it will have. Mark out several planes on the rhinoceros's hindquarters with the metal spatula.

9. Gently pat the model with a wooden slat to compact the surface without smoothing it, and to highlight the volume.

10. When building the head, place a mirror on one side to check the resemblance of the two halves and retouch if necessary.

11. Use the cutting wire to remove a section at the front and then at the back. Hollow out the animals through these two incisions.

12. View of the interior hollowed using a round modeling tool. Before this I have marked a 1 cm (³/8 in.) line in the exterior of the cut with a potter's needle.

13. Hollow out the hindquarters following the same procedure, making sure to maintain a uniform thickness. Also be careful not to pierce the wall. If this happens, the best way to rectify it is by covering it up with the surrounding body.

14. When the animal is hollowed out, do the same with the two sections that were removed.

15. Score the surface with the needle in the area cut and apply slip. Position the two pieces and connect them, making sure they fit together properly.

16. Use the needle to lute this area and place a small coil on top to seal the joint.

17. Use the wooden rib to press a little coil over the joint and smooth it down until it merges with the rest. This should result in a uniform surface on which no cuts or marks are visible.

18 and **19.** Views of the finished piece and after glazing.

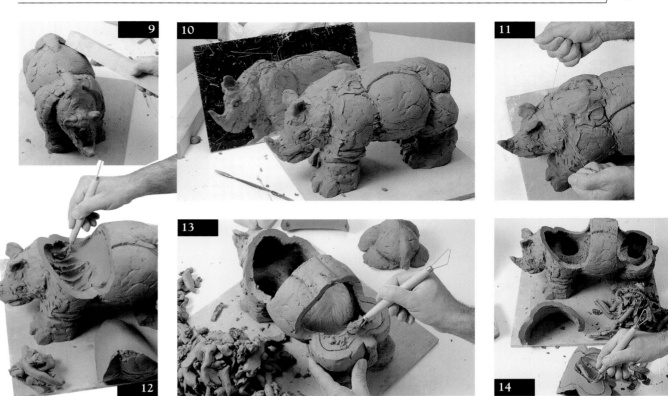

Joaquim Chavarria.
Rhinoceros, 1998.
34.5 x 20 x 38.5 cm
(13¹/2 x 7⁷/8 x 15¹/8 in.).
Firing temperature:
1280°C (2336°F).

GEOMETRIC SCULPTURE

The sculpture demonstrated here has been hand-built from a single chunk of clay. Medium-grain grog was used for this particular exercise. Because of the size and shape of this piece, it can be worked without inter-nal supports. The absence of an internal armature greatly eases the cutting and hollowing-out process, as will become evident in the steps below.

1. Here are the materials needed: stoneware ceramic body (two packages), wooden strip, looped modeling tool, metal rib, potter's needle, wooden slats, and round metal cutters. You'll also need a wooden mallet and a spray bottle.

2. With a strong movement, slam together the two packages of stoneware body.

3. Place the mass of ceramic body on the table and bang it down hard with the edge of the wooden slat, while beginning to bring out the form.

4. Place the piece upright and smack the top with the wood, gradually shaping the body.

5. Place the piece flat on the table and use a wooden mallet to build the sides.

6. With the strip of wood propped against your shoulder and resting on the table and angled against the clay, check to see if the sides are straight.

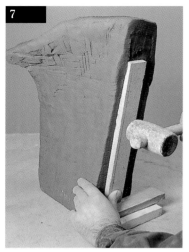

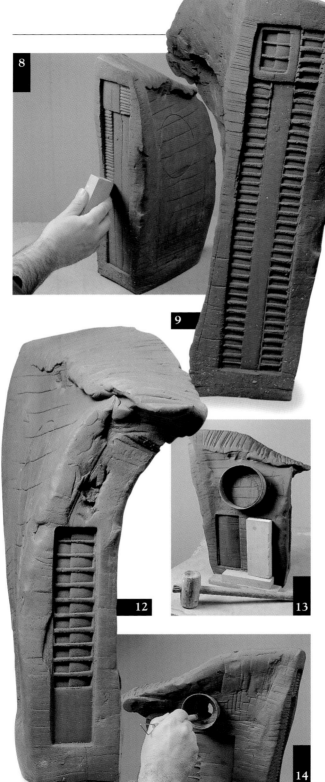

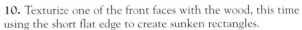

10. Texturize one of the front faces with the wood, this time using the short flat edge to create sunken rectangles.

11. View of the texturizing in progress.

12. View of the curved side with relief designs finished.

13. Begin adding textures to the second face. Insert a metal cutter but do not cut all the way through.

14. Insert a smaller metal cutter in the back and begin to empty it out in order to feed the wire through.

15. With the cutting wire held very taut and touching the edges of the metal cutters, remove all the surplus body, leaving a conical opening.

7. For decorative purposes, mark out a rectangle along one edge by pounding the wooden strip against the clay. The strip should be supported at the bottom by two pieces of wood so the base remains intact.

8. To give texture to the inside of the rectangle, make impressions with the edge of a piece of wood.

9. View of the finished side with small reliefs added.

16. Smooth down the inside of the cut with the scraper, taking care not to distort the shape.

17. View of the piece with the opening finished.

18. Score the edges with the potter's needle.

19. Prepare a wooden slat of about the same height as the lateral face.

20. Dampen the scored area with water from the spray bottle.

21. Begin to build the edge, joining small pieces of clay over it for a relief effect.

22. Carry out the same procedure on the top part of the piece.

23. To support the upper part, use a piece of wood to brace the overhang until the clay hardens somewhat.

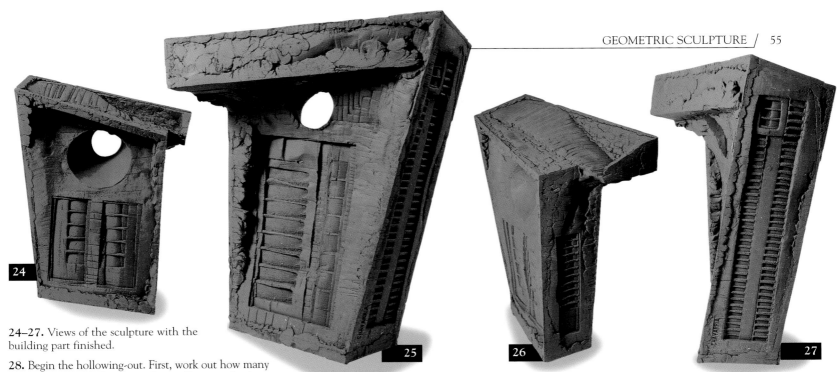

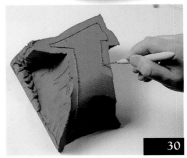

24–27. Views of the sculpture with the building part finished.

28. Begin the hollowing-out. First, work out how many incisions are needed in the sculpture. Remove the first part at the top using cutting wire.

29. View of the section cut.

30. Use the potter's needle to outline the contour to be hollowed out. Leave a thickness of about 12 mm ($^1/_2$ in.).

31. With the rounded modeling tool, mark out the area to be hollowed out. Scoop out ample clay with the rounded modeling tool. Use your thumb and index finger to check that the thickness of the walls is uniform.

32. Score the surface of the cut edge.

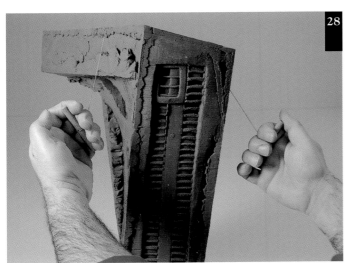

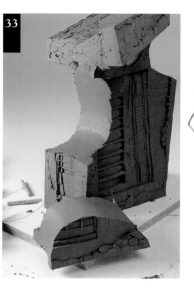

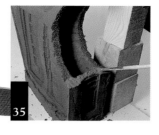

33. Cut the second portion and perform the same operation: mark the contour, then cut and remove the clay.

34. View of the sculpture with about two-thirds hollowed out. Note how the modeling tool enters through the cut and can be seen on the inside. Since this incision weakens the structure, I have used a wooden support while hollowing it out.

35. Score the contact zone and apply slip over it so the parts will adhere properly.

36. Begin to join the separate parts to the main body of the structure. Press them together gently with both hands to obtain a better join.

37. Lute the contact zone with a potter's needle.

38. Lute the joined parts and place a coil on top of the joint.

39. Use the modeling tool to smooth down the coil to reinforce the joint, taking great care not to penetrate between the scores of the luting.

40. To prevent the piece's shape from distorting, lay the sculpture on plastic placed over a layer of Styrofoam. With the needle, mark the last part that has to be hollowed out.

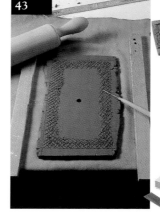

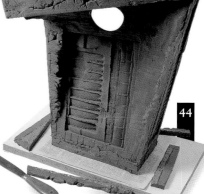

41. With the looped tool, remove the interior clay until the form is hollow. Then, with the scraper, cut the surplus material until you reach the perimeter.

42. When the sculpture is completely hollow, repeat the scoring operation in the contact zone.

43. Prepare a slab of body of the same thickness as the walls of the sculpture. Place the structure on top and mark out its perimeter. Score the interior and make a ventilation hole in this slab.

44. Spread slip over the contact areas of the sculpture and the slab and press them together carefully until the slip seeps out. Cut away the excess pieces of the base with a scraper. Lute the area with the needle, attach a coil, and smooth down the area. The structure is finished.

45. View of the sculpture after bisque-firing.

46 and **47.** Views of the sculpture after glazing is complete.

Joaquim Chavarria.
Blue on White, 1997.
44 x 34 x 19 cm (17¼ x 13⅜ x 7½ in.).
Firing temperature: 1280°C (2336°F).

ABSTRACT VOLUME WITH ARMATURE

*B*efore beginning to sculpt this type of work an interior framework, or armature, must first be prepared to support the clay during the hand-building process. Armatures are useful for building large sculptures and for sculptures with complex forms. This exercise uses several wooden slats and iron rods. Remember that the frame must be removed before the ceramic body hardens; otherwise it will not dry properly and will crack even before it is fired. In order for the support to be removed easily, the ceramic body must be extracted from around it while the work is being hollowed. It is essential to plan this operation so that the frame can be removed easily without damaging the piece. This exercise uses stoneware with medium-grain grog.

1. Fasten two strips of chipboard to the reverse side of the piece of chipboard so that it can be moved more easily. Place two square wooden slats perpendicularly on the top and fasten them with right-angle metal supports.

2. Wrap the right-angle supports and the slats with adhesive tape so that the ceramic body will not stick to them.

3. Cut a piece of ceramic body with a cutting wire and use it to form small pellets. Apply them to the base of one of the slats, pressing down in order to ensure they stick firmly.

4. Continue applying pellets while creating the volume that will give the general form. At this stage it is time to place the narrowest slats to augment the frame. Note that they are tied by a cord so they can be removed easily during the hollowing-out procedure.

5. Cover the entire frame with this stoneware with grog, continually building. Note that I have left the points of the slats uncovered; these I will cover in the second phase of building.

6. Detail of a fragment of a piece, from another angle. Before covering the top of the frame, place an iron rod 5 mm (3/16 in.) in diameter against the wooden slat. Push the rod about 15 cm (5 7/8 in.) into the body, and continue building using the pinch technique.

7. General view of the work before another rod is inserted in the second support, while building the lower part of the volume.

8. Detail of the rod in place. If it is too far into the body, lift it to adjust the height.

9. After covering the rod with ceramic body, finish off this part, using the slat as a guide. From this point on I will use different wooden slats to obtain various planes and straight volumes.

10. Another detail of the upper part of the volume as the work progresses.

11. To build the part that will serve as the joint between the two volumes, insert another iron rod and cover it with pinches of clay.

12. Using the wooden slat as a guide, finish modeling one of the lower lateral volumes of the sculpture. This view shows the work at a very advanced stage.

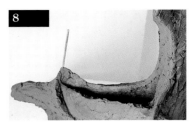

13. Following the same procedure, finish building the edge of one of the volumes, the area in the middle of the sculpture. A small wooden slat supports another larger one in the lower adjacent volume. Remove the wooden slat and the upper one comes away easily.

14. Use the potter's needle to score a small area on one of the volumes, on which to build another volume.

15. I have modeled this other volume separately and will join it with slip over the scored area. Here I am going over the surface with a saw, to make it uniform.

16. With the piece relatively complete, smooth over the surface with the saw without completely finishing it, which should wait until after it is hollowed. Let it harden for 24 hours.

17. The sculpture is now hard enough to be hollowed out with ease. Plan the areas to be cut; I begin first on a fragment at the top. It is important always to work from top to bottom.

18. With the potter's needle, outline the area to be removed. With a rounded modeling tool, begin to hollow out the piece. Remove the body surrounding the bar. Check now and again with your thumb and index finger to see if the thickness of the walls remains uniform.

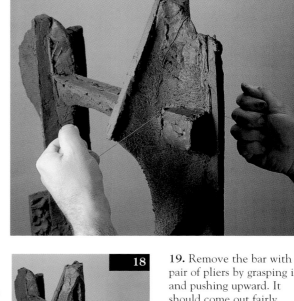

19. Remove the bar with a pair of pliers by grasping it and pushing upward. It should come out fairly easily, and the hole it leaves in the upper part can be covered with a pinch of ceramic body, or it can also be left as it is, as a ventilation hole.

20. Next cut another fragment, below the previous one. Hollow it out and connect it to the one above, then do the same with the fragment cut. Score the contact zone and apply slip on top. Join the two parts and lute them with the potter's needle.

21. Prepare a coil from clay extracted from inside the piece, and place it on top of the luted area.

22. Using a rib or similar modeling tool, press the coil down, making sure it penetrates between the scored lines to strengthen the joint. Smooth down the surface with the same tool.

23. Finish off the process with the saw, leaving the surface joined and without any apparent cut.

24. To close the top part, hold it gently with one hand and position it properly. Press down carefully with both hands until it is firmly in place.

25. After hollowing out the upper areas, continue cutting the middle part of the sculpture. Note that the lateral part has been cut in three places, one of which was explained in the previous step. Cut the cord that supports the slat and remove it using the pliers.

26. Score the area with the potter's needle and apply slip for a secure joint. Continue the same process until the entire sculpture is hollowed out.

27 and **28.** Views of the sculpture from two different angles. I have left the texture produced by the toothed scraper. The hollowed sculpture is finished and is now in the drying process, which must be slow. The holes at the bottom produced by the frame will provide the necessary ventilation.

Joaquim Chavarria. *Volume III,* 1998.
69.5 x 64 x 38.5 cm
(27¼ x 25¼ x 15⅛ in.).
Firing temperature: 1260°C (2300°F).

KILNS AND FIRING TECHNIQUES

An understanding of firing techniques is fundamental when getting involved in the art of ceramics. The various processes involving firing with wood have remained much the same as in ancient times. Methods range from firing over a simple bonfire, a method still in use, to pit firing and firing in various types of wood-fired kilns, which have taken different forms and have become more efficient over time. Wood-fired kilns basically consist of an enclosed space or container in which to put the piece to be fired, and a combustion chamber. Chinese, Korean, and Japanese potters constructed even more sophisticated kilns in the form of a long, partially buried tube placed on an incline, making use of sloping terrain. A fire was lit at the lower end of the tube so that it would rise naturally and fire the pieces placed inside the tube. The fire was ventilated by holes in the upper part and along the body of the kiln. Later, coal-fired kilns were introduced, followed by petroleum-fueled ones. Today the most commonly used types are electrical and gas-fueled kilns.

Packing the Kiln

How you stack the kiln will depend on the type of firing to be done. Thus, packing a kiln with raw pieces is different from packing it with bisque-fired, glazed pieces. Since this book covers only hand-building techniques and does not touch on glazing, it explains only the methods for stacking a kiln and firing raw pieces.

The pieces placed in the kiln should be completely dry. Before placing them in the kiln, think about how you are going to arrange them and whether bats and support columns will be necessary. You should have these on hand in various sizes. Bats can be placed on four support columns, but keep in mind that the maximum stability is gained by using three columns that coincide vertically throughout the levels. A logical way to stack the kiln is to put the heavier pieces on the base or floor of the kiln, and the lighter ones on the upper levels.

The pieces can be placed directly on the base and bats of the kiln, or may be stacked as long as the weight is evenly distrib-

View of a stacked kiln after bisque firing. Note the pyrometric cone placed on the bat so that it is just in front of the peephole in the kiln door.

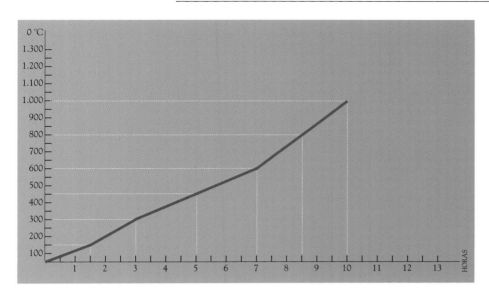

Graph of the bisque-firing process in an electric kiln. The final temperature reached is 1000°C (1832°F).

Each kiln comes equipped with a pyrometer, an instrument that measures the temperature inside the kiln. Pyrometers are very efficient, especially the electronic ones with digital displays.

Pyrometric cones allow potters to establish the temperature of the kiln precisely, as well as to determine the time-temperature ratio. The cones are made of ceramic materials designed to double over when they reach a certain temperature. They should be placed in the kiln so they are visible through the peephole when the door is closed. Place them on a lump of clay at an angle of about 8° so they bend as soon as the proper temperature is reached. The kiln should be switched off when the vertex of the cone touches the bat.

uted. Pieces should be placed far enough apart to allow the hot air to circulate freely around them. Some pieces can be placed inside others, as long as sufficient space is left so that they do not break when they shrink. If you are using an electric kiln, be sure to place the pieces at least 3 cm (1 1/8 in.) from the elements.

Firing

Firing takes time. Attempts to economize on time and on electricity or fuel can destroy a great deal of work and effort.

After loading the kiln, start off slowly, with a low temperature and all the air vents open to allow the water vapor to escape. The temperature should be increased slowly to at least 400°C (752°F). After this, you can accelerate the process somewhat until the temperature reaches 600°C (1112°F). Then the temperatures can be allowed to rise more quickly until the desired temperature is reached. In the case of low-temperature bisque firing, the peak temperature should be 900–1000°C (1652–1832°F). High-temperature bisque firing ranges from 1250 to 1300°C (2282–2372°F).

When the correct temperature is reached, switch off the kiln, which will produce a rapid fall in temperature that eventually stabilizes. Wait until the kiln reaches room temperature before opening it.

Measuring the temperature

It is important to control the kiln temperature as precisely as possible. This can be done using either a pyrometer or pyrometric cones.

Shaped like truncated pyramids, pyrometric cones are designed for a heating rate of 150°C (302°F) per hour.

GLOSSARY

Anhydrous. Compounds formed without water or from which all water has been removed.

Atom. The smallest particle of an element. Atoms combine to form molecules.

Bisque ware. Pottery that has only been fired once and is not yet glazed.

Bisque-firing. Preliminary firing to harden a piece before glazing.

Brush. Used in the glazing process to apply the glaze and decorate the piece. Slip can also be applied with a brush.

Calcination. Process in which a ceramic mineral or mixture is fired at a certain temperature.

Canvas. A strong cloth made of cotton or hemp.

Carpenter's square. Metal, wooden, or plastic tool in the form of a right angle (90°).

Clay. A substance made of hydrous alumina silicates. A particle of clay consists of one molecule of alumina (containing two atoms of aluminum and three of oxygen), two molecules of silica (one atom of silicon and two of oxygen), and two molecules of water (two atoms of hydrogen and one of oxygen).

Clay body. A mixture of various types of clay, minerals, and other, nonplastic materials.

Coil. Made rolling a ball of clay back and forth with the fingertips until it stretches out into a snakelike shape.

Contraction. *See* Shrinkage.

Cutter. Metal tools with sharp edges for cutting different shapes out of thin slabs of clay.

Diagonally cut. Cut at an oblique angle.

Element. A chemical substance that cannot be broken down into simpler substances.

Firing. Heating a clay object to a specific temperature.

Framework. Support around which ceramic body can be modeled.

Granite. Intrusive rock with a high silica content.

Hand-building. Manipulating plastic material to give it a specific shape.

Hollowing out. Technique of removing clay from a piece when it is still soft, before it has reached the leather-hard state.

Igneous or volcanic rocks. Formed from cooled and solidified magma and other igneous material. They are intrusive rocks if formed in the innermost layer of the Earth's mantle, cooled slowly, and they have compact grains.

Kneading. Manipulating clay body with the hands until it reaches the desired consistency.

Leather-hard clay. Partially dried and hardened clay, still containing some moisture.

Levigate. To dissolve a powdered substance in water. The finer particles remain in suspension while the larger ones settle to the bottom.

Limestone. A sedimentary rock composed of calcareous materials, containing more than 75 percent calcium carbonate.

Luting. Uniting two parts of a clay object by scoring with a potter's needle. The joint should be reinforced with a thin coil of clay pressed into place with a modeling tool.

Marble. Metamorphic rock essentially composed of calcium carbonate ($CaCO_3$).

Metamorphic rock. Formed from igneous or sedimentary rocks that have undergone structural and mineral changes principally caused by pressure, high temperatures, and chemical and recrystallization processes.

Modeling. *See* Hand-building.

Modeling tool. Metal loop in a wooden-handle; essential for hand-building in clay. Used to shape, refine, unite two parts, lute, smooth, texture, and more. The iron ones are used to work plaster as well.

Molecule. The smallest part of an element or compound that can exist in a free state.

Nepheline syenite. A variation of sodium-potassium feldspar that melts at a lower temperature than common feldspar, producing vitrified pieces.

Nonplastic. Having no plasticity.

Single firing. Firing a piece only once, with glaze, eliminating the bisque-firing stage.

Plaster slab. Used to absorb excess moisture from clay.

Plasticity. Quality of a clay that allows the particles to slide over one another and hence to keep a given shape.

Porosity. Capacity to absorb moisture or to allow it to evaporate.

Raw piece. An unfired piece.

Refractory. Highly resistant to melting and capable of withstanding high temperatures.

Rib. Modeling tool.

Rolling (the clay). Process used to prepare a slab by rolling clay out on a piece of canvas with a rolling pin to the thickness of wooden slats placed along either side of the clay.

Scoring. Scraping or cutting lines into a piece during modeling to reinforce a joint before painting it with slip.

Scraper. Serrated-edge tool used to cut clay or other ceramic body, as well as to smooth, score, or texture.

Sedimentary rock. Formed from igneous or metamorphic rocks that have been eroded by the elements.

Shrinkage. Contraction of clay body during the drying or firing processes.

Sieve. An fine-meshed implement through which powdered substances are passed.

Slab. A piece of clay that has been rolled flat and can be used to build certain types of pottery.

Slip. A watery clay mixture used to join parts of a piece before drying or firing, added during the hand-building process after hollowing out.

Smoothing. Evening off or polishing the surface of a dry or hardened piece using the appropriate tool.

Soluble. Able to be dissolved in water.

Spray bottle. A container with a handle that disperses water in a fine spray, used to moisten pieces during hand-building. A sponge can also be used, or simply sprinkle water on the piece with the hands.

Stacking (the kiln). Loading a kiln with raw or glazed pieces, distributing them appropriately so as not to obstruct the circulation of air during firing.

Stoneware. Glazed ceramic ware in which the clay and the glaze have completely fused to produce a vitrified, nonporous piece through firing at temperatures higher than 1200°C (2192°F).

Strips. Pieces cut from a slab of clay body; they should not be wider than 3 cm (1 1/8 in.).

Vitrify. To become like glass.

Warping. Distortion of a ceramic piece during drying.